# TAKING THE HIGH PLACES

## The Gospel's Triumph over Fear in Haiti

**TERRY SNOW** WITH **JEMIMAH WRIGHT**

P.O. BOX 55787    SEATTLE, WA 98155

YWAM Publishing is the publishing ministry of Youth With A Mission. Youth With A Mission (YWAM) is an international missionary organization of Christians from many denominations dedicated to presenting Jesus Christ to this generation. To this end, YWAM has focused its efforts in three main areas: (1) training and equipping believers for their part in fulfilling the Great Commission (Matthew 28:19), (2) personal evangelism, and (3) mercy ministry (medical and relief work).

For a free catalog of books and materials, call (425) 771-1153 or (800) 922-2143. Visit us online at www.ywampublishing.com.

**Taking the High Places: The Terry Snow Story**
Copyright © 2007 by Jemimah Wright

14  13  12  11  10      2  3  4  5  6

Published by YWAM Publishing
a ministry of Youth With A Mission
P.O. Box 55787, Seattle, WA 98155

ISBN-13: 978-1-57658-412-5
ISBN-10: 0-57658-412-7

Library of Congress Cataloging-in-Publication Data

Wright, Jemimah.
   Taking the high places: the Terry Snow story: the Gospel's triumph over fear in Haiti / Jemimah Wright
     p. cm.
   ISBN-13: 978-1-57658-412-5 (pbk.)
   ISBN-10: 1-57658-412-7 (pbk.)
   1. Snow, Terry. 2. Missionaries—Haiti—Biography. 3. Haiti—Politics and government—1986– I. Title.
   BV2848.H4S66 2007
   266.0092—dc22
   [B]                                        2007019037

# In Appreciation...

To my family:

I would like to express my warmest appreciation and love to Ingvild, my wonderful Norwegian wife. Through her constant encouragement and loving support I have been able to endure the race God has placed before me. I love you!

To my children, who have joined in the spiritual quest of taking the high places for Christ, I love you!

To YWAMers:

To all our YWAMers in Haiti and across the globe, who have run beside me for the cause of Christ in Haiti, I salute you. I extend my deepest appreciation for your sacrifice in taking the high places for Christ. May we never give up!

To intercessors:

This book only gives a glimpse of the effectiveness of intercessory prayer. To the intercessors who have prayed fervently through the many adversities mentioned in this book, God bless you!

To the author:

With my most heartfelt gratitude I extend my deepest appreciation to a marvelous woman of God, Jemimah Wright, for her incredible writing skills in bringing this story of Haiti to life. Her perseverance, patience, and determination to see this book to completion was commendable. Her investment of time, travel, and sleepless nights was beyond the call of duty and a blessing to me. Thank you so much, Jemimah!

Terry Snow

# Other International Adventures

*Adventures in Naked Faith*

*Against All Odds*

*Bruchko*

*A Cry from the Streets*

*Dayuma: Life Under Waorani Spears*

*Imprisoned in Iran*

*Living on the Devil's Doorstep*

*Lords of the Earth*

*The Man with the Bird on His Head*

*Peace Child*

*Tomorrow You Die*

*Torches of Joy*

*Totally Surrounded*

*Walking Miracle*

# Contents

# ONE

# Anger from the Lord

THE sound of something crashing to the floor woke me with a start. In the darkness I rolled over to look at the clock. It was two o'clock in the morning. I had been asleep for an hour. Since I was alone in the house, I immediately assumed an intruder was downstairs, but before I could jump out of bed, I suddenly felt God say, "Don't worry. It was just My angels."

Peace washed over me, and I went back to sleep.

The next morning all was well, and I e-mailed some prayer partners to tell them what had happened. I thought nothing of it until that evening when I checked my e-mails and Youth With A Mission (YWAM) India had responded. At the exact same time that I was awakened by the crashing downstairs, they had been having a prayer meeting. While they were praying for me, one of the DTS (Discipleship Training School) students had a vision of angels coming down from heaven and entering our home. There were so many angels that they were knocking things over. The student had seen the angels go out and set themselves up on the mountains surrounding the city. He didn't know what St. Marc looked like—or that mountains actually do surround our city.

I was greatly comforted by this picture of God's protection because Haiti, where we were living at that time, was in the middle of a civil war. My wife, Ingvild, and our five children had evacuated, along with most of the YWAM staff, but I had decided to stay with the people. I had said I would lay down my life for the gospel, but until then I had never experienced the reality of it.

The civil unrest of 2004 had come about under the presidency of Jean-Bertrand Aristide. Major gunfights were taking place between the rebels (the Cannibals) and the national police force. To make sure the Cannibals didn't take over St. Marc, Aristide depended on a gang called the Bale Wouze to control the city. He had to secure St. Marc from the Cannibals, who could have tried to capture the city before setting their sights on taking the capital, Port-au-Prince. The Bale Wouze (which means "clean sweep") were a politically active group that supported Aristide and were just as ruthless as the Cannibals.

The people in Portail Montrouis, the zone of St. Marc where the YWAM base was situated, were fearful for their lives. Non-Christians were asking me to preach the gospel to them.

"Of course," I replied with surprise. Never before had the lost asked me to preach to the lost.

I offered to open up the base and set up a sound system so that people could hear.

"No, no," they insisted. "We want you to come out on the streets." They said that if I preached inside the property, people might not come in, because they wouldn't feel worthy.

The people from our zone showed us where to set up a wooden stage under a street lamp—the only one that hadn't been shot out. I began to preach the gospel night after night. Each night when I asked whether anyone wanted to ask Jesus into his or her heart, everyone's hand went up.

One evening after preaching I began to feel very uneasy. Since I couldn't figure out why, I just said a prayer and went to bed. At one o'clock in the morning while I was sleeping, the Bale Wouze, led by a man named Samoza, came into our zone. Samoza was easy to identify, not only because of his great size and muscular build but also because both arms were tattooed with flames of fire from the shoulder all the way down to the wrist.

The Bale Wouze doused our stage with gasoline and burned it down. They then went to seven homes and set them on fire while the people were still in them. One family literally clawed through the cement walls out the back to escape with their lives. Samoza and his gang fired shots at them to make sure they couldn't come back to save their possessions. By a miracle nobody was killed or even injured, but the family lost everything.

The next morning when I woke up, I heard about what had happened. I was deeply saddened. I didn't rush right out. I felt I needed to have the heart of God first, so I went alone to pray. When I went into the zone, I was devastated by what I saw. Nothing was left but a charred image of where our stage had once stood. Homes were in ruins.

I went to meet the families of the burned houses. Showing me the holes they had crawled out of, they told me their stories of how they had scrambled to escape.

"That's where I had to stay while they shot at me," one man said, pointing toward the ocean. "I wanted to put out the fire, but they wouldn't let me."

I started to weep with the people for what had happened to them. I felt deeply their pain and devastation.

"What is to be done?" I cried out to God.

I felt God say that I had to go to the police and the Bale Wouze. (The police were working hand in hand with the Bale Wouze, turning a blind eye to the gang's attacks.) God said He would give me a word for them once I got there. Simmering with anger over what had happened to the people in the zone, I jumped into my truck with Pierre-Richard Charlotin, a Haitian YWAMer.

"God, help me forgive," I cried out.

"The anger you feel is from Me," God replied.

When we arrived at the police station, everyone came out. I felt God tell me to stand on the top of my truck. I stood up and screamed at the top of my lungs, "You touched my zone, you touched me, and therefore you touched my God. The judgment of God is coming. Repent!"

"What happened?" some of the police asked with confused expressions on their faces.

I then realized that a few of the police hadn't been involved.

"If you don't know what I am talking about, you have nothing to worry about, but if you do know what I am talking about, then hear this: you touched my zone, you touched me, and therefore you touched my God. The judgment of God is coming. Repent!"

Shaking with anger, I got back in the truck, and we drove to the Bale Wouze headquarters. Stopping the truck in the middle of the main road, I said the same thing. Everyone ran out to see what was going on. After I had said my piece, I got back into the truck and left.

We drove down to the South End police checkpoint, and I gave my message. Then we left the city. I had promised some clothes to people outside St. Marc, so we delivered a bundle or two of clothing and returned by the south entrance. As soon as we entered the gates, we were stopped.

"What's happening, Terry?" a policeman I knew asked.

I got out of the truck and repeated the message I had given before. The police wanted me to stay and talk with them, but I had nothing more to say.

As we drove on, I asked God which road to take and how fast to go. (This had become the norm for me. I knew that God would protect me. I just had to listen to and obey His voice.) Suddenly I felt God tell me that we needed to go back to the Bale Wouze headquarters and give the message again. I asked Pierre-Richard what he thought. He agreed, and we made a right turn toward the gang's headquarters. Again I stopped in the middle of the road by the Bale Wouze and shouted, "You touched me, you touched my zone, and therefore you touched my God. The judgment of God is coming. Repent!"

This time a whole crowd of people were present, all asking what was going on.

Samoza and his sidekick, a man they called Magistrat Ernest, appeared through the crowd. They began to mock me and laugh at what I was saying.

"You can say what you want, but God will have His way," I told them.

Samoza walked straight into my shoulder, spinning me around.

"I guess you've made your decision," I said, looking directly into his eyes.

He stared at me with intense anger. As I got back into the truck, Samoza and Magistrat Ernest started swearing, calling Pierre and me disgusting names. I got out of the truck and looked Samoza right in the face.

"You can cuss me out to my face, but don't cuss me out when my back is turned," I said sternly before getting back into the truck. I still don't know whether that was from God or was just the Texan spirit coming out in me.

As soon as I shut the door, the men again started swearing. Once more I got out of the truck.

"Cuss me out to my face, but don't wait until my back is turned," I said slowly.

I got back in the truck, and they started up again. This time when I went to turn the doorknob to get out, God put an impression in my mind of an action I was to take. It happened so instantaneously I didn't even think about it, which was a good thing.

A third time I got out of the truck. This time I knelt before Samoza and Ernest, placing my hands on my head.

"Do what you want with me, but it will not stop the judgment of God," I said.

Standing directly in front of me, Samoza pulled out a gun and pointed it at my head. I watched, as if in slow motion, the pistol come up. Out of the corner of my eye I could see Pierre-Richard turn and walk away.

*Here I come, God,* I prayed silently, but I didn't feel any fear.

Samoza placed his thumb on the hammer, and his finger on the trigger, and held the gun to my forehead. All of a sudden he dropped the gun and turned away.

I felt God say to get up and leave. I didn't need convincing. Calmly I got up and got into the truck with Pierre-Richard. A crowd of nearly three hundred people were now watching. I had to leave slowly because people were blocking the road. As I drove through the crowd, my heart began to race. I looked over at Pierre; his face was frozen, and he was staring straight ahead.

"What did I just do!" I exclaimed.

"He was going to kill you," Pierre shouted, his eyes wide.

"You left me!" I said with a smile.

"I told myself I was not going to see my director's head blown off, so I walked away," he said, shaking his head.

Adrenaline pumping through our bodies, and our hearts pounding, both of us were laughing and praising God. We knew that God had just saved our lives. It was only later that we realized the significance of what had just happened.

# Growth and Repentance

T H E sun was beginning to set as I rushed indoors from riding my horse, Goober. It was dinnertime, and I didn't want to be late. Tonight we were having my favorite meal—steak and mashed potatoes.

"Wash your hands," Mom shouted from the table.

I quickly cleaned up, combed my hair, and sat down next to my older sister, Shelly.

After Dad said grace I wolfed down the meal. Mom laughed at my appetite, but her mood was unusually solemn.

"I couldn't feel the keys on the piano when I was playing earlier today," she said suddenly.

I had begun to realize that my mother was not well. Always a vivacious and fun-loving woman, Mom tried to make light of the situation, but I saw her glance at Dad and saw the fear in her eyes. She was eventually diagnosed with multiple sclerosis (MS).

Three years after she found out she had MS, she was bedridden. One day I was at home watching TV when some people from church delivered a wheelchair for my mother to help her to get around. They wheeled it into her bedroom. When she saw it, she let out a terrifying scream, as if someone had been murdered. I turned away from the sound, trying not to hear. I was so scared and didn't know what to do. As Mom's disease got worse, our family slowly fell apart. She had been the nucleus of our family and the glue that held us all together.

My parents were both Christians, and all of their parents were Christians. My dad met my mother, Joyce, at Southwestern Bible College in Texas, and they married soon afterward.

My dad's father, the Reverend Latin E. Snow, was an Assemblies of God minister. He became a Christian when my dad was a teenager, and on his conversion he turned into a radical evangelist. His job was to fly over the rice fields of South Texas to survey irrigation canals. While he was flying he would look out for church steeples. If he couldn't see any in an area, he would later take his wife and my dad, Lester Lee Snow, and they would climb into their old Ford truck and start tent meetings in the area before planting a church.

I thus had a Christian heritage that I am thankful for. I had many experiences of God as a child and gave my life to the Lord many times, just to be on the safe side. But it wasn't until I was nineteen that I began to develop a real relationship with the Lord.

When I was thirteen, I began to turn away from the church and God. Shelly and I were in the youth group of Faith Assembly of God Church, Granbury. All the youth were involved in a play called *He Knew the Master.* Led by our pastor, Mike Riggins, we went on the road with the drama. This was something special. Shelly and I were excited by the praise we were all getting from neighboring towns. On the last night we returned to Granbury to perform at our own church. My mother was there. Even though it was getting more difficult for her to leave her bed, she had made a special effort to see her children perform.

As I stood on stage and looked out into the audience of familiar faces, I saw Mom in the back row. In our prayer time before the drama, I had felt God clearly speak to my heart, saying, "I am going to heal your mother if you will pray for her and lay hands on her. Only don't stop praying until she is totally healed."

My heart raced. Nothing could have made me happier than to see my mother well again. After the drama, I moved to the back of the church and knelt down behind Mom, putting my hands on her back. I cried out to God for her healing. Soon the whole room recognized that something was happening, and they started to pray, stretching their arms toward her. At one moment my mother stood up, which was amazing. I wanted to continue praying, and I felt God again say, "Keep on praying until she is completely healed."

I don't know how long I had been there, but after a while an elder from the church came over and lifted me up. He walked me to the men's washroom. Standing in front of the door he said, "That's enough for now, Terry. Get ahold of yourself and calm down." I was confused and upset. I didn't understand why they were stopping me. I had to pray more. Mom still wasn't healed.

Pastor Mike gave me a ride home. We sat in silence. Staring out of the window I watched the houses of Granbury by night. All seemed peaceful, the very opposite of the turmoil that was going on inside of me. Where was God? Why hadn't He healed my mother? Was He really there? I felt I had been made a fool of in front of everybody.

From that moment my life took a different direction. Being loud and outgoing, I had always been told to be quiet and behave. This trait became a hundred times worse when I turned away from God. I began to swear in a way that would have horrified my mother had she ever known.

I justified my actions by saying that a good Christian had to first be an experienced sinner. I began to push every part of my life to the limits. I wasn't alone. My sister Shelly, who was two years older, was going down the same path. As Mom slowly became more crippled with MS, my life that had once been so secure began to fall apart around me. The church that my grandfather had founded, and that I had grown up in, went through a messy split over doctrinal issues. I was too young to really understand, but it still had a negative impact on my life. At the age of fourteen I was drinking, taking speed, smoking marijuana, and going wild. Since I did everything with 100 percent heart, I put my all into fighting, wrecking cars, and staying out late.

My mother was bedridden by this time, and she wasn't aware of what was happening. My father, the head chemist for the Miller beer company, spent more and more time at the office, as home life had become harder for him to deal with.

When I was about sixteen, I went with a group of my friends to a Halloween carnival. We were all half drunk and having a lot of fun being loud and messing around. As we sat on the tailgate of my pickup truck, passing around the alcohol, out of the corner of my eye I saw people I recognized: Pastor Riggins and my old youth group. They were at the carnival sheepishly trying to share their faith with people and pray with anyone who wanted prayer. I laughed at them and silently said to God, *If You ever save me, may I not be like them, but may I be bold and coura- geous and go to the most difficult places and the most difficult people.* Lit- tle did I know that God was listening to my drunken prayer.

Suddenly bored, I got up to leave. I jumped into my prized possession—my green Ford truck. Dad had bought it for $1,000 when I turned sixteen. He said he didn't want to buy me anything good, as I would surely just trash it. He was right. I crashed the truck many times, but I had fun doing it.

During this time I was still going to high school, attending just enough days to get by. Miraculously, I graduated and went to Lincoln Technical Institute in Dallas to study mechanics. I lived in an apartment with another student from the college, and the same pattern I had relied on in high school became the norm—attending just enough classes to get by and graduate.

May 8, 1983, was my nineteenth birthday. I wasn't due to graduate until June 1. To celebrate the fact that I could now legally drink, I bought two barrels of beer with some friends. We were drunk for three days. It was during this time that I totaled my truck by driving into a telephone pole one Sunday night. The police found me after crashing the truck and arrested me for driving while intoxicated (DWI). I ended up in jail. My only worry was that I had to be at school on Monday morning or I would not graduate. I needed to complete my attendance quota.

I phoned my dad, and he called the judge, asking for mercy. They let me out, and Dad drove me back to Dallas in time to make my class. He was very disappointed in me. This was one of many times he had gotten me out of trouble. Later he told me that I looked so bad when he saw me that he felt no need to yell at me. We drove two and a half hours to Dallas in silence.

Back in Dallas my prospects were not good. I now had no vehicle and no job. One afternoon I was walking along the road, making my way to the theater to see a movie. I had nothing else to do, and no ambition to find something to do. As I was walking, I suddenly felt the conviction of God.

"Repent," He said clearly.

I got goose bumps all over but kept on walking.

*I'll go to church on Sunday and repent,* I reasoned with the voice.

I had arrived at the theater by this time, but I felt God say, "Don't go in. Don't buy the ticket."

*This is crazy,* I thought, but by this time I was shaking. Ignoring the feeling, I bought the ticket and sat down to watch the movie, thinking I would ask for forgiveness after the movie had ended. Still shaking, I could feel the conviction of God still heavy on me. Then all of a sudden, the voice I had been hearing stopped. Panic filled me. Had God given up on me as I had ignored His voice to repent at that moment? Had I committed the unpardonable sin (Matthew 12:31–32)?

My shaking increased, and I rushed out of the theater and made my way back to my apartment. Collapsing onto the floor, I dragged myself to my bedroom, in case my roommate came in and saw me. I knelt down at my bed, crying to God, asking for another chance, forcing the tears to come. There was only silence.

I had blown it. I was doomed to hell. By that evening I was in such a state that I was contemplating suicide. As I was considering this, from the very depths of me came the smallest voice: "There *is* still hope." Holding onto this, I made a plan. *Okay, God, I am going to live a righteous life. I am going to be so good that You are going to have to forgive me.*

For the next few days I continued to shake and was noticeably pale. My friends got angry with me, thinking I was keeping some great drugs from them. They would not believe the truth. I had stopped drinking and taking drugs.

Ten days later on June 1, I graduated and went home to Granbury. I continued to ask God for forgiveness, but by then I had begun to hear a voice that said no, and the voice continued to say no. In desperation I decided that if God wasn't going to forgive me, then fine. I would go and get so drunk that I would kill myself. If I was going to hell anyway, I might as well have one final wingding, I thought.

The day of my decision I was at the gas station filling up my dad's car. I ran into my sister's friend from youth group, Stormie Brannon. We started talking, and Stormie invited me to a revival meeting that night. After much persuasion on her part, I finally agreed, but only if she would come and pick me up. Stormie came late, and I was cross at her for that. After all, I didn't have all night. I wanted to go and get drunk.

We eventually arrived at the Church of God in Granbury, a small church with only about sixty people. We sat on the old wooden pews. I gripped ahold of the side of the pew, trying to disguise my shaking, but the vibrations of my body went into the seat, which rattled against the linoleum floor from the shaking. Stormie gave me a sideways glance, wondering what was wrong with me. I sat listening to the preacher. It seemed like everything he said was what I had said to God.

"Some of you have said to God that you are going to lead such a righteous life that He will have to forgive you," he said.

I was dumbfounded. Was God trying to speak to me? At the end of the service people were called to the front to repent. I rushed forward, hoping I was being given another chance. One last time I cried, "God, will You forgive me?"

The pastor came to pray with me, and I began to weep. The "no" that I had been hearing was growing fainter. Finally the voice was quiet. I knew I had been forgiven. At that moment the shaking completely stopped.

I went back to my seat, but suddenly the preacher pointed to me. "Son, God isn't finished with you yet," he said. He told me to lift my hands toward heaven. As I did so, what felt like a heavy backpack fell from my back. At the same time I had a vision of heaven. I saw a man cheering at the throne of God saying, "Father, I knew he would come to us! I knew he would make it!" Then I saw an arm come down from heaven and take hold of my wrist. "This is the strongest bond. I will never let you go," I felt God say.

The preacher's voice came into my hearing. He was happily saying, "That's it!" I realized I was speaking in some foreign tongue and could not stop my mouth from jabbering. This went on for about fifteen minutes. Afterward all the bad language that I had been so famous for, and that I had tried so hard in my own strength to stop, left.

What I understood after reflecting on this time was that the "no" I had been hearing was the voice of Satan. I had so let him into my life that his voice was the predominant one I heard. I now understood why my righteous living was not appealing to God. His salvation cannot be earned by works.

My first words from the altar were, "I must go tell." I went to my beer buddies and got them to stop the delinquent things they were doing. We started played miniature golf instead of fighting and drinking. It was quite a change.

My family noticed something more than a change in my attitude. They said that my whole physical appearance changed after I got home from the revival meeting. My parents phoned my sister, who was now living in Arlington, Texas, to ask her what was going on with me. She didn't know, but she was so curious that she came to Granbury to see for herself. God was working in Shelly as well, and a week or so later, Shelly rededicated her life to the Lord.

With my change in lifestyle I started going to church again. I explained what had happened to me, but many were still cautious, wondering whether I would again start leading the youth astray. Within two weeks my life became the church. Every evening was filled. I didn't want to do anything else. I became active in the youth group simply because I was bored at home just watching TV.

I got a mechanics job in Granbury, but it didn't fulfill me. I asked God for direction so that I would know what to do next. One morning as I was praying before work, I felt God speak. "On Sunday you will know." That was all I heard. Nothing more.

Full of expectation I woke up the following Sunday morning and went to church, straining to hear what God was saying. I wondered when or how He would speak to me. I waited. Nothing.

Back at home I sat on my bed, listening to the birds singing outside, trying to hear the voice of God tell me to go somewhere or do something. Suddenly the quiet was disturbed by the ringing of the telephone. It was Stormie, wanting to know if Shelly and I would go to a drama that she and some friends were putting on that night. She was on her outreach from a Discipleship Training School (DTS) with some organization called Youth With A Mission (YWAM) in Tyler, a town three hours from Granbury.

At first I said no, thinking I had to go to the evening church service to hear God. But Stormie and my sister pressed me, and I gave in.

*If You are going to speak to me, God, I guess You can speak anywhere,*
I prayed.

I arrived at the drama and met Stormie's YWAM friends.

"This is Terry. He is going to do a DTS." That was Stormie's only introduction. Whatever a DTS was, I wasn't thinking about doing it. I was busy trying to hear God's voice for my future. At the end of the evening I still had not heard God. Feeling dejected, I went to Stormie's house with my sister. *Why haven't You spoken to me? You said that today I would know what You wanted me to do,* I cried out to God. At that moment Stormie's introduction came flooding back into my ears: "This is Terry. He is going to do a DTS." Suddenly it was as though a light had switched on in my head. It was obvious. God wanted me to do a DTS. Excitedly I started planning to go to YWAM.

A few days later Poppy Hatcher, my mom's dad, phoned to formally invite me to dinner. This was unusual since I often went to my grand-parents' house for meals, just turning up, never with a formal invite. Poppy had a big impact on my life growing up. He was a man of integrity. Always faithful to the Lord, he never seemed to waver. Poppy was a butcher by trade but had also, with his wife, Frances, started a church in Granbury.

As I drove up the driveway to the house, I saw my grandfather waiting for me on the porch. I smiled when I saw him, this Texan wearing his uniform cowboy hat, boots, and belt buckle. He looked up and waved. I always knew that Poppy loved me.

Over dinner Poppy told me how a couple of months ago he had been praying for me and Shelly. He had told God that he could do nothing more with us and was surrendering us into His hands. It was then that God had started to move in my life. Poppy said that God had told him that I would need some money to do something. I told him I was thinking of joining YWAM. Poppy said he would check it out first. We scheduled time to visit the base in Tyler. Poppy was pleased with what he saw and paid my fees in full. I applied to do a DTS course in January 1984. I had no idea what would happen, only that God was showing me His path for my life.

# THREE

# Learning to Hear His Voice

I ARRIVED on a chilly Saturday afternoon in January at the YWAM ranch in Tyler. The next day the Discipleship Training School was beginning, and I was excited. I had made an effort with my appearance and had put my best flannel shirt on my skinny frame. My tool cap and my skin-tight Wranglers tucked into my cowboy boots made it clear to everyone at the YWAM base that I was a Texan through and through.

While at trade school in Dallas I had lived in an apartment with one other person. Now I would be sharing a room with seven other guys on beds that were three bunks high. I was shown to my dorm, and the first roommate I met was Mike Wood from Mobile, Alabama. Mike had recently become a Christian and was now zealous for the Lord. He had pinned a poster on the door of our room saying "Pray for Revival!" At first I cringed when I heard him coming along the corridor. Every time he came through the door he would slap the poster and say, "We need to pray for revival!" I had never seen anything like it.

Another Texan, Bo Bolding, shared the room. Bo was an East Texan from Kilgore. He was a bit older than I was and very studious. I couldn't relate. Ernie, the oldest in the room, came up to me with his hand outstretched. "Hello. My name is Ernie, and I am called to be an apostle." Speechless, I shook his hand. What do you say to that? Somehow I didn't think I was going to fit in.

My saving grace in the dorm was Chris Huston from New Mexico. We were the same age and had a similar outlook on life.

The first night of the school we had what was called a family night. Leland Paris, the director, got up and said, "Some people have come to this DTS in the past not knowing it was a mission training program. They came here thinking it was something else." He was describing me exactly.

I thought I was just attending some type of glorified Bible camp. I had come because God had told me to. I had no idea what I was getting into.

Leland explained more. "A DTS is a five-month missions program split into three months of lecture and two months of outreach to another country." I decided I would finish the school, but I had no plans to become a missionary.

I formed two relationships in my months at DTS that have impacted my life greatly. The first was with my small-group leader, Stew Bauman. Before I met Stew, I had heard he was from Canada. I had assumed that because it was so cold in Canada, everyone who lived there must be an Eskimo. I was a nineteen-year-old Texan, dumb to the world. After all, why would a Texan need to know anything else about the world when he was already living in the center of the universe? I had hardly ever been out of the state. Once, while on the church drama tour, we had gone as far as Mississippi, but I hadn't even realized that we had left Texas.

It was somewhat of a shock to be surrounded by people from all over the country and from other nations. After two weeks of "We need to pray for revival" and "I'm an apostle," I wasn't feeling very comfortable. It didn't help that in my own state of Texas I was laughed at by the other American "foreigners" for the way I dressed.

At mealtime someone always prayed before we ate. I was used to hearing Poppy pray "God, bless this food to the nourishment of our bodies. Amen." But these people would get up and start interceding for the world. It made me feel as though I didn't know how to pray—and that maybe I didn't even know who God was.

One afternoon I was walking with Stew on the grounds of the ranch. "I don't think I belong here, Stew," I said.

Stew looked at me, and I carried on. "I just don't fit in here. I can't be like these guys that I live with. They all seem so superspiritual. I'm just a guy from Granbury, Texas. It wasn't all that long ago that I was hanging out with my friends getting drunk. I didn't even know this was a missions program."

Stew laughed and put his hand on my shoulder. "You know, Terry, I think you may have your head on straighter than some of the other guys here. So don't worry about it."

That gave me enough encouragement to stick around for a bit longer.

In DTS I did learn to hear the voice of God above everything else. I had heard God speak before, of course, but at DTS I learned to identify His voice. I began to pray, "Lord, I want to hear Your voice in every circumstance and in every situation."

One day during my prayer time I asked God to speak to me right there so that I would know that He was the one speaking. I felt God say, "Get up, walk out the door, and walk to the parking lot by the gymnasium."

The gym was only about a block away. I thought I would try it out, just in case it was God. As I reached the parking lot I saw an old Ford truck driving up the road. Suddenly I heard a bang and a splutter, and the truck broke down right in front of me. The driver jumped out of the truck, panic on his face.

"Can you help me out?" he asked. "Something's wrong with the shifter. I can't figure it out, and I am in a real hurry," he said.

"Sure," I replied.

It just so happened that the truck was a similar model to my old one, and I knew immediately what the problem was. I popped open the hood and fixed the shifter, and the guy went on his way.

*Wow,* I thought. *Maybe that was really God.* I asked again, "God, where else do You want me to go? What else do You want me to do?"

I felt Him say, "Go up to the boardwalk." This was an area on the ranch where we had our classrooms. As I stepped onto the wooden boardwalk, Kathy Agen, one of the DTS students, came charging out of one of the rooms. Almost hitting me with the door, she did a double take when she realized it was me standing there looking straight at her.

"Thank goodness you are here, Terry!" she exclaimed.

*That's nice,* I thought.

"I need you right now to be measured for your costume for the outreach drama. I need it all done by supper."

I was amazed at God—that He would speak to *me,* and so clearly. Learning to recognize His voice guided me through many difficult times that were to come. God was training me by helping me listen in the small things.

The highlight of hearing God's voice during my DTS was when it came time for outreach. The staff asked all the students to pray about where they felt they should go. They gave us three locations: Guatemala, Honduras, and El Salvador. I prayed, and I felt that God told me El Salvador.

The staff collected our papers that we had written our country on, at the same time saying, "Now, you might not get to go to the country you want, but that doesn't mean you missed God."

*What does it mean then,* I thought!

The next day, all the students were called together to hear where they would be going. "Terry, you are going to be going to Guatemala," I was told.

I was so confused and disappointed. I went to Stew and told him I really felt God had told me El Salvador. He explained that the country was very volatile at that time, and they didn't want just anybody going in. They had picked only people who they felt were mature.

"So I guess that means I'm not mature," I smiled. "But I know God has told me I am to go to El Salvador."

Stew left to pray about it. He came back and said, "Terry, I know you feel that God told you to go to El Salvador, but I think He is saying He wants me to invite you to come with me to Honduras."

Honduras was a hot spot at the time too. I decided to pray and ask God what to do. Clear as a bell I heard God tell me, "You are going to El Salvador, but accept Stew's offer to go to Honduras."

I went back and told Stew. I then had to rush off to get a passport, as I would need one for Honduras. Several weeks later, when we were all sitting in class, we heard this announcement: "The Honduras outreach has been cancelled due to situations out of our control. All those going on that outreach have been teamed up with the El Salvador team."

I just looked at Stew, sitting in the corner of the room. He caught my eye, and we both smiled. "Stew, I told you!"

"You sure did," he laughed.

Stew was one person who dared to believe that I, a crazy cowboy, could hear the voice of God.

One night after hearing a challenging message on how I had to surrender all for the cause of Christ, I went into the empty prayer room to be alone and pray. I was feeling troubled. On my knees I cried out to God, "You want all my life, but You couldn't even heal my mother. You made me look like a fool in front of all those people. You dropped me. How can I surrender my life to You? You don't even care."

I figured God knew my feelings, so there was no point trying to hide them from Him. All of a sudden I felt God speak to my heart. "I weep for your mother, and I wept the day that happened."

In my hurt and frustration I cried out, "What! The God who can heal my mother is weeping. Big stinking deal."

God said, "Would you like to know how I feel for your mother?"

"Yes," I replied.

I felt God say, "I will give you My heart, but the moment it is too much, say so, and I will remove it from you."

Immediately God hit me, and it was like someone had punched me in the stomach. Tears started streaming out of me. I could not contain them. It was as if the wind had been knocked out of me, I felt so much pain.

"Enough!" I cried out in tears. Immediately the tears and pain left. "I believe You weep for my mother, Lord, but I don't understand why You didn't heal her."

God never told me why He didn't heal her, but He did show me that He cared.

I made one friendship in my DTS that I didn't realize until later would be so important in my life. It was with a lovely Norwegian young woman named Ingvild Synnøve Edskerud. About a week after our DTS started, Ingvild showed up. She had arrived late because of visa difficulties and was taken straight to class. Everyone had heard that someone was coming from Oslo, Norway. All I knew about Oslo was that it was where all American children's letters to Santa Claus were sent.

Ingvild came into the classroom. She had short brown hair styled in a bob, and beautiful brown eyes. She sat right behind me. I turned around with a big smile, and in my thick Texan accent I said: "Howdy. Welcome to Texas!" When I didn't get much of a response, I continued, "I guess you don't understand English too much. That's okay. You'll get the hang of it."

Ingvild just looked at me, and I could see she was thinking, *Who is this strange person speaking to me in a language I don't understand?* She was not yet fluent in English, and later I found out that with my accent she had not understood a word I had said. That was the end of our relationship in DTS. She had her friends, and I had mine.

During DTS I asked God if He had a woman in mind for me from the school to be my wife. I had broken up with my girlfriend from Granbury because she wasn't called to the mission field. I knew by now that God was calling me to other countries after my DTS. God replied as clear as day, "Yes, I have someone for you."

"Who, God, who?" I questioned excitedly.

"Someone you would never think of," He said.

I thought that was crazy, since I could just go through the list of women on the DTS and find someone. I went through the whole list, and God was right. I didn't even consider Ingvild. This was mainly because she didn't speak much English, and in a school of about sixty students, we just didn't connect. So that was the end of that, I thought.

After DTS I did a School of Evangelism (SOE) and then stayed on at the Tyler YWAM base to help lead other schools. In May 1985 I was chosen to staff a DTS outreach to a little country in the Caribbean called Haiti.

# FOUR

# Never to Come
# Back Again

OUTSIDE the window it was raining and already dark as we began our descent into Port-au-Prince. The air that met me as I stepped off the plane was hot and humid. I held tightly to the rail of the steps down to the tarmac below. I was trying hard to ignore a growing feeling of apprehension. What would this island of Haiti be like?

Sixty-five other young people were on the trip. We were going to separate into three groups to work on different projects for a few weeks before traveling on to the Dominican Republic for the rest of the outreach. I would be coleading one of the groups working at an orphanage.

Tired and sticky, my group piled into a waiting bus that had been organized by Mark Brock and Bill Landis, the outreach leaders. Without thinking, we put our luggage on the roof of the bus, only to find after arriving at the orphanage an hour and a half later that all our clothes were soaking wet from the rain. We had nothing dry to sleep in.

We stopped after a bumpy ride in an area just outside Port-au-Prince called Carrefour, where my team would be working. We unloaded the bus in the dark, trying to make out the place we were staying through the shadows of the night. The rain had stopped by this time, and we stumbled to our "bedrooms." The ten women slept on the cement floor of a church owned by the orphanage. This was like a palace compared to the shed that the men were placed in. As I lay in my wet clothes on the dirt floor under a tin roof, with ants biting my neck, I hoped I would never again have to come back to this miserable country.

The sun shining through the cracks in the wall greeted me as I opened my eyes the next morning. Still hot and sweaty, I was in desperate need of a shower. Looking around I saw that the room did not look any better in the light of day. Out of the corner of my eye I saw something moving above my head. A huge rat was hanging from the rafters. I stifled a scream of shock, and then with an accepting smile, as if this is what should be expected, I thought to myself, *Welcome to Haiti!*

Avoiding the rat, I sheepishly stepped over my sleeping teammates. Making my way to the shower I found there was no water to wash with. I made it through the day, drying my clothes and getting used to the very new surroundings. The water distribution truck arrived late in the day, and I eagerly headed back to the shower. It was basic, with cement walls and no windows, but I expected that. What I did not expect was for nothing to come out of the showerhead but a surge of air. Then suddenly, before I could get out of the way, a swarm of mosquitoes gushed out and imbedded themselves into my chest. The water that followed smelled so bad that I was better off before the shower than after it.

We had heard some of the history of Haiti from missionaries who had passed through the YWAM base in Texas. On the plane I had read through my notes again. Haiti shares the Caribbean island of Hispaniola with the Dominican Republic. It was first inhabited by the native Arawak Amerindians, who were discovered by Columbus in 1492 but were killed off by Spanish settlers. In the early seventeenth century, the French established a presence on Hispaniola, and in 1697, after bloody battles, Spain ceded the western third of the island—Haiti—to France. The French colony, based on forestry and sugar-related industries, became one of the wealthiest in the Caribbean, earning the title "The Ruby of the Caribbean," but only through the heavy importation of African slaves and considerable environmental degradation. According to verbal history, on August 14, 1791, a black slave and witch doctor named Boukman led the slaves in a voodoo ritual. They sacrificed a pig and drank its blood to form a pact with the devil, whereby they agreed to serve the spirits of the island for two hundred years in exchange for freedom from the French. The slave rebellion, under Toussaint L'Ouverture, started on August 22, 1791. After thirteen years of conflict, the slaves won their independence. On January 1, 1804, they declared Haiti the world's first independent black republic.

Knowing this, I wasn't too excited to learn that five voodoo temples were situated around the orphanage where we worked. The people gave us constant headaches, banging their drums all through the night. One morning as I was walking around the area praying, I passed one of the temples and asked God whether I should go in and pray. As I looked up, I saw a man sitting in the doorway of the building beckoning me in. I went in, looked around, and prayed. Later when I returned to the orphanage, I told the other team members what had happened. They asked if they could go and pray there too.

The next morning, accompanied by ten students, I returned to continue praying. This time the voodoo priest showed up. He started mocking us and making fun of our prayers. This made me angry. I warned the man, "Don't mock—God will have His way." I challenged him to repent and turn to God, but he only laughed. We left soon after that, and nothing obvious seemed to have happened to the priest or his temple.

The team continued to help at the orphanage. We worked in the garden and cleaned out the cesspit, not a job I relished. There was a problem with the cistern that no one could figure out until we looked inside, where we found the orphanage's beloved pet rabbit rotting away. This explained the foul-smelling shower water, again confirming to me that this country was not for me.

The end of our time in Haiti didn't come a day too soon. I now knew where I was not called to go and was excited to be moving on to our next outreach location, Santo Domingo, the capital city of the Dominican Republic. Everything went well in Santo Domingo, and I thought perhaps God would call me to a Latin country to work for Him.

After three weeks in the Dominican Republic, it was time to return to the YWAM base in Tyler, with its three hundred acres of ranch land and showers that plumbed mosquito-free hot water. I stayed on at the Tyler base and started looking at the different nations in the world. Where would God send me? Haiti was totally out of my mind.

When I returned to Tyler I decided to join the Caribbean mobile team founded by Bill Landis. A mobile team is a group of people with a common vision for a cause or country. It is launched from a geographical YWAM campus that will support the vision and goal of the team. The Caribbean mobile team was created for the purpose of promoting the expansion of YWAM throughout the Caribbean.

A year quickly passed and I was still in Tyler. The mobile team was planning its first mission trip. The three islands for outreach were Grenada, Trinidad, and Haiti. Since the team would split up into three smaller teams, I prayed about where I should go, and I thought I heard a small voice say "Haiti." Because of my past experience in Haiti, I dismissed this as not from God. I continued praying, but I couldn't hear anything else.

Later that day the leaders of the Caribbean mobile team met to decide who would lead which smaller team where. There were five of us: Bill Landis, Bob Emberly, Kim Cook, Craig Cunningham, and me. We all sat on the floor of a church we were visiting, and each person said what he felt God was saying. For some reason I was the first to speak. I said I wasn't sure, and that I hadn't heard God on which country to go to. Craig was next. He looked at me and smiled. "I don't know where I am supposed to go, but I think God told me where Terry is to go." Kim said the same thing.

"Do you want to tell us where you are going, or shall we ask them?" Bob asked, smiling. Squirming uncomfortably, I remembered that tiny thought I'd had earlier in my time of prayer. "I suppose, if I had to say anything, I guess it would have to be Haiti." There was no excitement in my voice, but as I mentioned Haiti, the others who had heard from God for me all jumped up laughing. God had told each of them that I was to go to Haiti. With that confirmation I knew I had to obey, but I certainly was not pleased about it.

The summer of 1986 I took my second mission trip to Haiti. I was the leader of the outreach, and at twenty-one years of age I felt very inadequate. We had a small team of eight people, including Brian Shipley and Julie Emberly. This time my experience was more positive. We worked in partnership with Buddy Johnson and Cecil Pitman of Feed the Children, and I felt we were useful to them and got things accomplished.

I had a chance to go back to the orphanage we had worked at the year before. This time there were only four voodoo temples surrounding its borders. I asked what had happened to the temple we had prayed in. We found out from various sources that the voodoo priest's son had gone out onto the road and been run over by a car and died. The priest had later died in the same way when he was drunk. The people in the area had concluded that the temple must be a cursed voodoo temple and had torn it down. I shivered and recalled my words: *God will not be mocked.*

On the last day of the trip I felt a sense of relief that I had led my first outreach team and it had gone well. I was eager and excited to go home. I still had no glowing compassion for Haiti and kept on telling myself, "Almost over, and never to come back again."

That evening the team met after our meal to pray with Buddy and Cecil. I asked them what they would have us pray for.

"Pray for more laborers," they replied.

Happily I agreed, thinking, *I am a YWAMer. I can pray this prayer!* Full of zeal, faith, and determination I prayed with all my heart, "God send forth more laborers!" But as I finished, again I heard that still small voice.

"You!"

"Oh no! Not me, Lord." I melted into my seat, then dropped to the floor on my knees. *Could this be God's call for me?* I knew in my heart what He was asking me to do.

The next morning we flew out early to Miami, where our group met the other teams that had gone to Grenada and Trinidad. We had fun catching up and exchanging stories of the things God had done. A bus was waiting to take us on the twenty-four-hour journey back to Tyler.

As people began to fall asleep, I moved to the front to sit by Bill Landis, who was driving.

"Something happened to me in Haiti, Bill, and I have to tell you I am leaving YWAM."

Bill saw that I was serious and asked why I was leaving.

"I have to leave YWAM because I think God has called me to Haiti." Since YWAM didn't have a base in Haiti, I assumed that I would have to join another mission. Bill did not think the same way I did.

"You don't have to leave YWAM. You can start YWAM Haiti!"

"Really?" I asked with surprise.

I could not believe that I, an inexperienced twenty-one-year-old, would be entrusted with starting a YWAM work for Haiti. What if I messed up? I knew I was far from perfect. I had no idea how to start, and I told Bill my reservations. Laughing, Bill reminded me that God was in this and He would help me. "Terry, if you feel like God has called you to Haiti, it must be God, because I know no one, especially you, who would choose to go there for any other reason!"

# FIVE

# Laying the Foundation

BACK at YWAM Tyler I told the rest of the Caribbean mobile team that I felt God had called me specifically to Haiti. To my surprise three others, Brian Shipley, Julie Emberly, and Mary Morrison felt that God had called them to Haiti as well. Like me they had thought they would have to leave YWAM to work there. Instead of leaving, however, we formed the new Haiti mobile team in the summer of 1986.

Our first desire was to get to Haiti as soon as possible. In November 1986 the four of us did our first official outreach to the nation of Haiti. We went to serve other missionaries, hoping to learn the ropes and find out the needs of the Haitian people.

Cecil Pitman, whom I had worked with before, asked us if we would go up to the tiny village of Ferrier in the mountains above Port-au-Prince at the end of a road. The four of us camped out on the mountain at night, and in the day we went door to door talking to the people and praying with them. On the first morning we met together to pray. God gave Mary a scripture from Zechariah 8:9–13. The passage was about laying the foundations in the land, that the island would become a blessing to other nations. We all felt that God was telling us He wanted us to start laying the foundations in Haiti, and we adopted the scripture as the theme passage for YWAM Haiti. We had no idea what work this would entail or the adventure it would take us on.

After a month in Haiti the team returned to the United States. Back in Tyler we had to figure out what we were going to do as a new mobile team. We had no finances, no vehicle, and no idea how to get started.

At an evening meeting at the Tyler ranch our team was commissioned. Leland Paris, the base director, called me up. "We are going to pray over Terry Snow and the Haiti team. This team is going to be launching a base in Haiti in one year."

*A base!* I thought with surprise. That was news to me.

With that thought ringing in my ears, I headed with the mobile team to different churches around the country to raise support for what we wanted to do in Haiti. YWAM Tyler supported us by giving us contacts and helping us recruit more members for the team from different DTS and SOE schools. Their leadership and guidance was invaluable to us.

In 1987, in our first year as an official mobile team, we did another outreach to Haiti. We went back up to the mountains of Ferrier where God had first spoken to us. As we were going door to door, we ran into some people at an intersection—nothing more than a mountain trail that split in two directions. We began sharing the gospel with them. A young man was listening in to what we were saying. As we finished sharing the gospel, we asked the people if anyone wanted to accept Christ. Each person had a different excuse and said no. But a young man named Blanco stepped up and asked if he could accept Christ. We led him in a sinner's prayer. Blanco bonded with us immediately and began to go door to door with us, listening to everything we had to say. Later he asked if we had a Bible to give him, but we didn't have any Bibles in Creole. We left the mountains during that outreach feeling sad that we couldn't give Blanco a Bible.

With the birth of the Haiti mobile team came another exciting change in my life. God had told me in my DTS that my wife was in the school, but it wasn't until two years later that He spoke again. It was during an outreach to Guatemala with Bill Landis that things began to happen. Bill had invited me to join him as final training before the Haiti mobile team started. One day I was sitting with him in a restaurant in front of a picture window, going over parts of the outreach. Ingvild was on the same team. As Bill was talking with me, Ingvild walked past the picture window. It was almost as if a light shined on her. God spoke to my heart. "That is the woman I have given you."

Bill kept talking, but I wasn't listening. I kept watching Ingvild. After that I arranged to have her sit with me in the car everywhere the team went. I always saved the front seat next to me for her. I wanted to get to know her.

From talking with her I learned that she had no idea what she was going to do with the rest of her life. At twenty-two years of age she was at a crossroads and didn't know whether to go back to Norway and then to school or to stay in Youth With A Mission. Since I didn't want to tell her I liked her while she was making such a big decision, I chose to keep my mouth shut.

A couple of weeks later Ingvild returned to Norway and prayed about her future. She again applied for a visa, saying, "God, if You want me back in Texas, You can give me the visa or close the door." The U.S. consulate not only gave her a visa but also gave her a lifetime multiple-entry visa, which was very rare. Ingvild came back to YWAM Tyler knowing that God was opening the door for her to be a missionary.

The problem now for me was that we hardly ever saw each other. By this time I was traveling a lot, and Ingvild was working on the Tyler ranch. Over time my feelings for her had subsided. I released her to God and told Him I would go along with whatever He wanted.

One day as I was driving to the gym at the Tyler base, I saw Ingvild walking along the road. As I watched her, God said, "I haven't forgotten."

My feelings for Ingvild started to reawaken. My twenty-third birthday was approaching, and I came up with a plan to be alone with her. The next day I sought her out. I started by making small talk and then eventually said, "It's my birthday on May 8. Would you go out with me?"

Ingvild said okay. I had very little money at the time, but I took her out to a really nice restaurant. For a missionary it was extremely expensive, but I wanted to give her the best. I was sure that after this she would get the hint that I liked her. After the meal I didn't sense that she had gotten any kind of hint. And I had spent a lot of money.

*Maybe she's not even interested in me,* I thought.

I vented my frustration on Stew, who said I needed to tell her how I felt.

Ingvild's birthday was only twelve days later, on the twentieth of May. When I asked her what she was doing for her birthday, she said she didn't have any plans. I invited her to the same restaurant. I wanted her to see I was trying to say something here! I spent all the money I had, nearly two months' support, to take her out again.

I went over to where she was staying to pick her up. Dressed beautifully in a tan-colored top and long skirt, she looked gorgeous. We ate our meal, and still I didn't think she was getting the hint. She wasn't giving me any clues that she was even remotely interested in me. Later I found myself sitting in a room with her. I tried to communicate how I felt, but my attempt was a disaster. I couldn't do it. We ended up having a pillow fight, throwing stuffed animals at each other.

The next day Stew drove up to me and through the open car window said, "Did you talk to her?" Glumly I replied, "No, I think I must have missed God. She doesn't seem interested in me at all."

He stopped me. "You're chicken! I can't believe you, Terry. You're yella!" He shouted those last words as he stepped on the accelerator and left me standing in the parking lot in shock. This friend—this Canadian pacifist friend—had called me yellow! To a Texan this was an outrage!

Then I started to think. I had just learned that Ingvild was in Stew's wife Gloria's small group, and I wondered whether maybe Stew knew something I didn't. Hope filled my heart.

At that time we were getting ready for a festival called "Jesus Go-Fest" in Texas. I was in charge of getting posters out. As a leader I made sure that Ingvild was in my vehicle. I arranged to drop everyone else along the road to leave Ingvild and me alone together in the van. We drove around in the old Volkswagen while the teams were out distributing posters. I was trying to figure out how to tell this woman I liked her and yet was feeling an incredible fear of rejection.

Finally we were sitting in the parking lot, waiting for the teams to return. We hadn't spoken much, because I could hardly breathe. Then

I saw that the teams were coming back. I thought, *If I don't tell her now, I don't know when I will ever tell her, and if I don't tell her today, Stew is going to ridicule me.*

With so much pressure I was getting more and more nervous. Ingvild probably thought I was hyperventilating.

"Ing…Ingv…Ingvild!"

Just before everyone got in the van, I blurted out, "I really like you!"

The team piled into the van, and Ingvild and I could just look at each other. Everyone had been talking and laughing before they got in the van. All of a sudden they sensed the atmosphere and stopped talking. Ingvild sat quietly, not saying anything. I was stuck driving for twenty-five minutes with eight other people in the van, unable to ask her how she felt. A perfect example of how not to ask a girl if she likes you.

We finally got back to the ranch. Very gently and carefully Ingvild told me that she liked me too. I was overjoyed. Ingvild had told God many years before that she would not look for a husband. She asked God that the one He had chosen for her would pursue her without any encouragement on her part. That would be how she would know he was the right one.

Once the words started falling, they flowed, and we talked for hours. We told Fran and Leland Paris and the other leaders what was happening. They advised us to make an announcement to the whole base in a week's time. I was soon to go on an outreach, and as I sat with Ingvild one afternoon, I simply said, "I know you are the one God wants me to marry. Will you be my wife?" She said yes. God had told her that she was going to meet a man, he was going to be a leader, and she was to follow him wherever he went. And He showed her that I was that man.

A week later, to Fran's amazement, instead of announcing our new relationship, we announced our engagement. Five months later, on October 10, 1987, we were married in the church my grandfather started in Granbury. For our honeymoon we went to Disney World in Florida, borrowing my grandfather's truck to get there. We then went to Norway for two months so that I could meet Ingvild's family.

We returned to Texas in January 1988 to prepare for the next DTS. Stew Bauman had invited us to join him in coleading the DTS in an attempt to keep a focus on Haiti and hopefully recruit some students to join us full-time. It all went well, and we recruited about twelve students. After that we were able to do an extended outreach to Haiti.

One day I started thinking about how we were going to prepare the foundations in Haiti as it says in Zechariah 8. I suddenly realized that a key was to plant the Word of God. I began to do some research and found out that only forty thousand Creole Bibles were coming in to Haiti per year to meet the needs of the then 6.2 million people. The Bible was not being planted. As I continued to research, I learned that it was 1985 before both the Old and New Testaments had been translated into Creole, the native language of Haiti.

"This is where we need to begin," I said. We came up with a campaign to raise money. We asked people to give ten dollars to have a Creole Bible purchased and hand-delivered by one of us to a person in Haiti. It was a big hit. We were able to raise enough money to purchase 150 Bibles and pay our way to Haiti with our new recruits.

We went back to the mountains of Ferrier. We had been told that there was no point handing out Bibles, as the people would just sell them for food. A Bible was worth a month's salary at that time. But we didn't just go door to door handing out Bibles. We spent a minimum of twenty to thirty minutes in each home. We put value in the Bible, so much so that people began to see it as a prized possession.

I remembered the young man named Blanco, whom we had met in the mountains, and briefed the teams to tell me if they met him. Sure enough, at the intersection where we had first seen Blanco, one of our teams met a man matching his description.

"What is your name?" they asked.

"Blanco," he replied.

Excitedly they said they had a Bible for him and asked if he was still a Christian. He said yes he was still a Christian. As soon as he got the Bible, he said, "Now I can go preach." He took it and ran rapidly down the mountain path. That was not the last time we heard of Blanco.

We continued through the mountains distributing Bibles for the next few weeks.

One time a friend and I were coming to the end of a long day of sharing the gospel. We had one Bible left. All of a sudden a little old woman from the very top of the mountain began to shout at us. She wanted us to come to her home. We were extremely tired, but we mustered up the strength and went up the mountain path to her house.

When we reached her door, she immediately cut down a refreshing piece of sugar cane to give us and took us inside her simple home. The house had a palm-leaf roof thatched and woven together, a single window, and walls made of sticks and plastered with mud. A simple bed and some chairs were inside. The woman was a gracious hostess, and we began to talk to her.

"Can you please give me a Bible?" she asked.

"Are you sure you want a Bible? Can you even read?" I inquired.

"No, I can't read. But if I can just open the Bible up at night, lay it next to my head or put it under my pillow, I know that God will be with me and will protect me," she responded.

We were amazed at this woman's faith, but we didn't want to hand out Bibles where they would not be read. We wanted to be sure that if we handed out a Bible, someone in the household would read it. I asked her if there was any way that a family member or someone she knew would come and read to her from the Bible. All her family members were dead, and she was all by herself.

"Does anyone come up here and visit you?" I asked.

"There is one man. His name is Blanco. He comes up and tells me about Jesus. He can read the Bible to me," she replied.

We left her a Bible, amazed at what Blanco was doing.

As we went on from house to house, the story was the same. Blanco had been there before us, sharing the gospel and reading his Bible to people. Over the past year he had been preaching even though he didn't have a Bible. He had laid a foundation for our team. He had only heard the gospel from us, and a year later we had found he had grown in Christ and in his relationship with God. Even though he didn't have his own Bible, he was proclaiming God's love to the people in that village.

One day while working in Ferrier, Brian Shipley was going door to door. He went into one home where a blind man lived. The blind man asked if Brian could give him a Bible. Brian replied, "But you can't see, you can't read the Bible. What good is it for you?"

"If you pray for me, I know God will heal me and I will be able to read and to see the Bible," he answered.

"You want us to pray for God to heal your eyes?" Brian asked.

"Yes," the blind man answered.

Brian and the translator laid their hands on the man. Brian later told me, "I prayed every prayer I could think of with all the faith I could muster up. I prayed until I didn't know what else to pray." And then Brian stepped back and asked the man, "Can you see?"

"Yes," the man replied.

Brian was shocked and overwhelmed. Could this be? He held up his fingers and asked the man how many he was holding up. The man could see how many. Brian was astonished that God had healed this man right before his eyes. He had never seen a healing miracle and never thought he would be used in such a way. But as he was obedient, going door to door, planting the word of God to the mountain people, God used him to bring sight to the blind. Brian became a key leader in YWAM Haiti, and God used Brian's gift of teaching to open the eyes of many Haitians to Jesus Christ.

On returning to Tyler we looked for different ways to tell people what we were doing and to ask for their support. We began to do youth lock-ins, where we connected with church youth groups and trained them in drama, giving them some basic Christian principles. This sharpened our skills in teaching and discipling and made us more effective leaders. As parents began to see how God was using us to change their children's lives, it became easier for them to believe that God would use us to make a difference in Haiti. However, it hadn't started well. Our first lock-in was disastrous. The youth were out of control, and we were pulling our hair out. In the end, the church gave us twenty-five dollars for Haiti. That didn't even cover gas. It was a sad day.

Because we knew that the lock-in idea was from God, we continued to try to perfect it. Eventually we saw some incredible results. We would show up at a church on a Thursday, and on Friday we would come together and arrange our schedule. We would then go back to our host home to get some rest before the evening. The youth began to arrive at about six o'clock for the lock-in. As soon as they arrived, we kept them busy. We gave them teachings on the character of God, their destiny, and relationships. We normally taught a minimum of twelve dramas, with lots of games and other activities. By three o'clock in the morning, the kids were worn out and ready to take a break. Later in the morning we would teach them how to have a quality personal devotion time and then would give them time to have it. We would meet together in small groups in which the youth would talk about what God was doing in their lives and what their struggles were. We would then pray with them. By the end of the lock-in, the youth were transformed. One youth pastor said, "You have accomplished in thirty-six hours what it would have taken me three months to do. How did you do it?" My answer was, we *didn't* accomplish great things in that time. *God* did.

On Sunday the youth would join us in ministering to their own congregation. They would present dramas, and we would share about the vision of Haiti. People were challenged by God as they saw their young people change.

The following summer in 1989 we returned to Haiti. This time we didn't only go to the mountains of Ferrier. We spent the majority of time in the slums of Port-au-Prince, in a place called Citi Soleil, where the poorest of the poor lived. Citi Soleil had no plumbing or clean water. Raw sewage filtered down canals into the ocean.

We were introduced to a wonderful couple. Jacques and Gladys Fourcande had a ministry right in the middle of Citi Soleil on a piece of land that was given to them by the government to look after the homeless children in the area. They invited us to come down and do door-to-door ministry. We said we would love to, but we didn't have a place to stay. I asked if we could we stay at the orphanage. Jacques and Gladys looked at each other in shock and then looked at me.

"You want to live there?" they asked.

"We'd like to live there, if it's okay, depending on how much it costs," I replied.

Jacques told us that if we wanted to stay there, we could stay for free. He tried to dissuade us, saying it would be too hard for us to stay there. The orphanage was on the edge of a canal filled with raw sewage, with no running water and only intermittent electricity.

I said we still wanted to go. Gladys and Jacques agreed, thinking we would stay only one night. We ended staying for the entire three weeks of the outreach. It felt like three months.

At night the mosquitoes would come out in swarms. They were so thick you could feel them bouncing off you as you walked. It was so hot during that summer in Citi Soleil that at night as you lay down to sleep, the perspiration would bead up and then dribble down across your body, as if somebody were pouring hot water on your chest. It was like sleeping in an oven.

We were down there with our team of twelve, including Ingvild and our now three-month-old firstborn child, Wayne Gideon. God protected us, but we would still wake up in the morning covered with mosquito bites. It was horrendous. Music would be blaring all night long—voodoo music and rock music from a nearby disco. We would get up early after not much sleep and begin our prayer and worship. Day after day we went door to door throughout the whole area of Citi Soleil, sharing the gospel and giving out Bibles. Once again people were healed and were saved.

One day we visited a woman with a fever. "Pray for me. I'm sick," she said.

We prayed for her and gave her a Bible.

"I believe God has healed you," I said as we left.

We then continued going door to door. When we finished about two hours later, we came back along the same trail and saw the woman up and cooking.

"Are you feeling better? What happened?" I asked.

"You prayed for me, and I am healed," the woman replied matter-of-factly.

Healings were so common at that time. We saw people being touched continuously.

We gave a Bible to another woman, and the next day while passing her house I noticed she had a bandage on her wrist. I asked her what had happened. She said she had gotten into a fight. I asked if she had forgiven the woman she'd had the fight with.

"No, I didn't forgive her. She threw a rock at me," she replied defiantly.

"Where's your Bible?" I asked.

"It's in the house," she said.

I asked her to get it, and I opened it to Matthew 6:14, where Jesus tells us to forgive those who have trespassed against us or our heavenly Father will not forgive us. I felt God nudge me to have her read the verse, and I handed her the Bible. I asked her to read the scripture and tell me what it said. She refused.

"I'm waiting," I said. "I am not going to leave here until you have read this scripture to me." Finally she read it. As she read it, her eyes began to fill with tears and she wept. God was doing something powerful in her.

"You must forgive people who sin against you," I said.

"Okay," she replied, "I forgive."

God was using us to teach basic principles and to lay biblical foundations. The weary team returned home from a fruitful time of outreach. That was the toughest summer we had ever had. We had some glorious reports and had faced some incredible challenges. It had been day-to-day survival, but it was all readying us for what God had for us in the future—learning to understand the people of Haiti and to know God's heart for the nation.

The Haiti mobile continued to grow. We had been going to Haiti for nearly four years, and I wondered what the future held.

# Outside the
# Promised Land

W A K I N G up early on a cold and clear January morning back in Texas, I decided to go for a walk and spend time with God. As I was walking around the ranch praying, suddenly God's presence appeared. I felt Him say, "I've given you a property in Haiti. You will receive a letter today concerning the property I have already given you."

This came completely out of the blue—I was just having one-on-one time with God. I wasn't asking Him to speak to me about the future, and I certainly wasn't thinking of moving to Haiti anytime soon. So when the impression came to me, I tried to get it out of my mind and focus on God, but God spoke again very clearly.

"I AM who I AM is speaking to you," He said.

As a young boy I'd had a Sunday school teacher named Betty Taylor, who had told us the Bible story of when Samuel began to hear God's voice and of how God had spoken to Moses. Sister Betty had explained, "Children, if you ever wonder whether you are hearing God's voice, you will know it's His if He says 'I AM who I AM is speaking to you.'"

Since I had never before heard God speak to me in this way, it really got my attention. I asked God what He had to say to me. He said the same thing: "I have given you a property in Haiti. You will receive a letter today concerning the property I have already given you."

"Okay, Lord, I receive Your word," I said.

As soon as I acknowledged God and told Him I had received His word, I was flooded with peace. I went straight to check my mailbox, but when I got to the mail room, the box had nothing in it; it was completely empty. I was confused. I was so sure that I had heard God. His voice had seemed so clear.

"Sometimes you hear God, sometimes you don't," I said to myself with a shrug.

I walked on to my morning meeting, kicking the dust under my feet. I met Stew Bauman at the door.

"Hey, Terry, here's your mail. I thought you might want it," he said.

Stew had gone to get all the mail for the base that morning. As he was sorting it, he had decided to take my letters and give them to me at the meeting.

I quickly started thumbing through the small handful of mail. One letter stood out because it was in a green envelope. It was from a ministry that I had never heard of before. I opened it quickly, wondering whether this was the letter God was talking about. The letter contained only two paragraphs. It said that their mission was getting rid of some property in Haiti. They knew I was working with YWAM in Haiti, they respected YWAM, and they wondered whether we wanted the property—for free.

I couldn't believe what I was reading. I started to shake. I told the leaders what had happened, and they asked me to tell the story at the base Sunday-night meeting, which I did.

Early the following morning, I laughed to see YWAMers walking in the same spot where I had told them God had spoken to me. They were all hoping that God would speak to them.

My leaders all marveled at God's clear direction for the mobile team. We contacted the ministry, and Fran Paris, Mark Brock, Kim Kaufman, and I went to St. Marc in Haiti to see the property. Once we got there we found the building was very run down. It reeked of urine, its walls were dark and murky, and it had voodoo trinkets all around it.

"Is this supposed to be a blessing or a curse?" Kim asked.

"Oh, this is a blessing; it's awesome," I said.

"You see something I don't see," she replied jokingly.

In my mind's eye I could see how it could become a place of training and equipping. I was very excited, but there was some bad news. The ministry told us that they couldn't find the legal paperwork to pass the property to us, but if we wanted it, we could have it.

At that time YWAM International was having some land disputes in different countries because YWAMers, in their zeal, had bought properties without the proper legal paperwork and were now having court battles over land.

Looking at these factors, our leadership wisely advised us not to take the property without the correct legal paperwork. I was confused. God had said that He had given me the property. Fran patiently replied, "If it is from God, He will sort it out."

I went away to pray about what I should do. God clearly said, "Move to St. Marc. I have given you a property."

I told the Haiti mobile team that we had to be obedient and try to start a YWAM center in St. Marc. We made plans, and we geared everything to move in 1991. The focus of our road trips changed from asking "Would you like to sponsor us to go to minister in Haiti?" to "We are starting a YWAM work in Haiti. Will you help us?"

Brian and a pregnant Cheryl Shipley were the first to move with their young son Josiah in January 1991. The rest of us would come down in June. The idea was that the Shipleys would get a foothold in St. Marc while everyone else did one final fundraiser.

First I would fly into Port-au-Prince with Brian. I helped him pack all his worldly possessions onto American Airlines pallets. "You realize we don't have a house. We don't even have a place to sleep tonight, and you are loading up everything you own to go. Are you sure you want to do this?" I asked him.

Brian just looked at me. "God told us to go to Haiti, didn't He? We're going."

I admired his complete faith in God.

We got on the plane. Twenty-four hours after arriving in Haiti, we ran into a missionary named Ray Thomas in St. Marc. Ray introduced us to Julie Dalencourt, a woman from an influential family in St. Marc. The Dalencourts ended up renting us a house on the northeast side of the city. The only challenge was that the house wasn't quite finished, but the Dalencourts promised that it would be ready no later than June. Until that time Brian and his family would live with Ray and Vivienne Thomas, the missionary couple who had introduced us to the Dalencourts. The Thomases lived just outside of St. Marc in a little town called Montrious.

When we first arrived in St. Marc, we had told Ray about the property we had thought God had given us. In his typically relaxed manner Ray said, "You don't need a deed. Just go ahead and occupy it. No one is going to say anything to you—this is Haiti!"

We were stunned by this but thought we would give it a go. Ray, Brian, and I went back to the property and met the guardian at the gate. The guardian asked who I was.

"My name is Terry." The guardian looked shocked. "*You're* Terry? Oh, come on in." He showed us the place and gave us the name of the lawyer in Port-au-Prince who was responsible for it. We immediately set off for the two-hour ride to Port-au-Prince to see the lawyer.

A stern-looking receptionist at the lawyer's office asked for our names and whether we had an appointment.

"No, ma'am, we don't have an appointment, but my name is Terry. I am here about the property in St. Marc," I replied.

"He is very busy, but I will tell him you are here," she said and left the room.

As quickly as she had gone, she returned, again asking, "Your name is *Terry?*" When I said yes again, she told me the lawyer would be right out.

Coming out of his office, the lawyer looked at me with confusion. "No, you're not Terry. You can't be Terry." With a smile on my face, but feeling slightly exasperated, I said yet again, "Yes! I *am* Terry—Terry Snow."

It suddenly dawned on the lawyer. "Oh! You are Terry *Snow,* not Terry *Nelson.* Terry Nelson is working out things in relation to the property you are asking about."

We found out that Terry Nelson had a ministry in Carrefour called Light Ministries. As we hadn't responded about the property, we figured that it must have been given to this missionary, who had found a way to secure the deed. I happily went over to meet Terry Nelson. Excitedly I told him the whole story about God speaking to me about the property. I was sure he was going to surrender the property to us.

Instead Terry looked at me and said, "You're nuts! Do you have any idea what I had to go through to secure that property from the thieves who were trying to take it? I had to pay $10,000 to back-pay the teachers and pay the lawyers."

I was dumbfounded. I walked out of the meeting like a puppy with my tail between my legs.

I went to God and asked what He wanted me to do. He told me to go back to Terry and ask again. I went back. This time with even more sincerity and emotion, I told him the story and asked again if he would give up the property. He still thought I was crazy. "In fact, in a couple of months we will be moving there ourselves," he said.

Tired and discouraged I went home and sank into a chair. I felt like I had blown it. I prayed that if God ever gave me another chance to have the property, I would trust in Him and not in man. I felt like the children of Israel must have felt when they saw the giants living in the land God had given them. Instead of looking to God and believing His word, they were afraid. The result was that they were not allowed to go into the promised land but had to walk around the mountain.

From this we learned that although it is important to submit to our leaders and come under their authority, if God tells us to do something, we have to obey.

Months turned into years, and Light Ministries still had not moved into the property. We carried on, using the small rented property on the northeast side of St. Marc as our base. We had no water and only intermittent electricity. My family stayed in an apartment where the bathroom was so small you could sit on the toilet and throw up in the sink. The shower was made of cement, and the kitchen was like a walk-in closet with cardboard boxes as kitchen cabinets. Rats were everywhere, and scorpions were coming in all the time.

For years we lived this way. All through this period I would pray, "God, You have to give us a place!" God always responded, "I have given you a place. Call Terry."

I ended up calling Terry many times over almost a seven-year period. One time we were in the airport flying back to the United States on the same plane. Terry sat on the far side of the room waiting for the plane to be boarded. I imagined he was hoping that I wouldn't come over and again ask him, "Terry, are you *sure* you aren't supposed to give us that property?" I decided to let him be that time.

For the next six and a half years I dealt with my guilt. I felt I had stopped the ministry from walking into the bounty God had promised us.

In 1995 Ingvild and I had attended a conference in America. While there, different people had prophesied over us. One woman said, "The property God has given you is sitting abandoned because you have chosen to abandon it."

That was the truth. I knew I had abandoned the property in my heart. My attempts to contact Terry were always halfhearted. I doubted that God was able to give us the property.

The property had never been occupied for the entire six and one-half years. Light Ministries had tried to do all they could to move in, but everything had failed. They would bring materials to start up a team, and the materials would be stolen. They would send people to secure the property and develop relationships in the community, but the people would leave after a month. Something would always happen. One man had a car accident; another had the front gate fall on him. Terry Nelson did all he could to take care of the property and start a ministry there, but it seemed like it just wasn't meant to be.

Meanwhile God had kept saying to me, "You have chosen to abandon the property. I see you as the owner. I will not let anything happen on the property because you have chosen to abandon it, and therefore it will be abandoned."

I was so frustrated. By this time fifteen staff members were living at the rented house, and they were going mad in such a small space. We needed something bigger.

Near the end of the seven years a man named Mike Smith visited our base. He was a pastor with whom we had developed a relationship over the mobile-team years. He had gone back into business and now ran a car dealership in Paducah, Kentucky. When he came to see the ministry, he saw how we were living and looked at our vehicles.

"These trucks belong in a junkyard, Terry. I had no idea how bad the situation was."

I shrugged and smiled. "Yeah, but we've got 330,000 miles on that blue Ford van. God is faithful!"

During his stay, Mike sat down with me. "Terry, have you ever thought God would want you to get a property of your own?"

*Oh brother!* I thought. But I took him around to a few properties in St. Marc that I, in my desperation, had thought perhaps we could use. Many times I had said to God, "Okay, God, I am going to go out and find a property, and You are going to *have* to bless it, because we just can't live this way."

God had always replied, "I have already given you a property."

I showed Mike all the buildings. At the last one, he said to me, "But, Terry, is there one property that stands out above the rest?"

Reluctantly I showed him Terry Nelson's property on Rue Maurepas. By this time tension between Light Ministries and YWAM was high. Terry was sick of me continually asking for the property. Because of this I told Mike I couldn't take him inside. We sat outside, and I told him the history. As I finished the story with a sigh, Mike simply said, "Call him."

At first I refused, but Mike was insistent. Without any hope I called Terry Nelson. Mike had a word of wisdom on how to communicate with him, and it worked. Terry Nelson said, "Let's talk."

That happened in late November of 1997, after nearly seven years of waiting. With Mike's assistance and after several conversations, Terry and I signed a contract for the property. Terry gave it to us for free but asked that we pay back what he had invested in the property. He asked for $100,000. We agreed to pay a deposit of $10,000 and were given a year to pay the balance and secure the deed to the property. If we could not do this, we would be able to back out of the deal, and Light Ministries would keep the $10,000 and consider it as rent for the year.

As soon as I left the meeting, I phoned Mike in Kentucky. Jubilantly I told him what had happened. While I was talking to Mike, it suddenly dawned on me. "I don't have $10,000!" I blurted out to Mike.

Calmly Mike replied, "Call your bank, Terry, and ask them for wiring instructions, and I'll wire you the $10,000."

My mouth dropped open.

In January 1998 a very happy YWAM staff moved into the long-awaited property on Rue Maurepas. During the six and a half years in our previous home we had been mocked and laughed at and had over $10,000 worth of property stolen from us. Our building had just been rocks and cement, no plants or grass. Our new base had a beautiful field of green grass. My heart filled with joy as I watched the staff roaming the field, enjoying it to the full.

At our first worship service I kept touching the walls, asking myself if it was a dream. For the moment I wasn't even thinking about how we would come up with the $90,000. We were on our property. That was enough.

# SEVEN

# Walk by Faith, Not by Sight

I HEARD the thunder crack just as I was drifting off to sleep. This was followed by the rain.

*I hope the staff will be okay,* I thought to myself. They had all moved onto the property, but I was still living in a house nearby with my family. I wondered whether the roof of the property, which had a few holes in it, would keep the rain from leaking into the building.

Early the next morning I made my way over to the base. I was greeted by staff running around looking like drowned rats.

"What happened?" I asked Louis Wells, one of the staff members.

"Rainwater came through the roof into our dorm room. Water was pouring through the roof more than it poured off it. The stairs turned into a waterfall. All twenty-two of us were huddled in the office downstairs trying to get some rest before the sun came up," Louis said.

We all worked together to fix things up, but I knew something more had to be done. *Help us, Lord,* I prayed as I worked. God turned the situation into a blessing. It introduced us to Paul Martin from Lititz,

Pennsylvania. Paul's daughter was in YWAM and was living at the Tyler ranch. Paul had taken a team of workers to build a youth center on the base. Fran Paris had seen what he was doing and was impressed with the team's work.

"This is incredible how your men are doing such good work, and so fast," she said. "If only we had more teams like you to go down and help people like Terry Snow in Haiti."

When Paul asked why, Fran told him about our roof problem. That night Paul woke up in the middle of the night. He couldn't sleep, thinking of us all under our leaky roof. Over the next few days it kept bothering him. Finally he felt God say, "Go and do something about it!"

Paul called me up to ask for the measurements. Since I had no idea how to measure a roof, he flew in for twenty-four hours to look at the roof and figure out the materials he would need to fix it. He prayed all the way home to Pennsylvania, saying, *God, I don't know what to do. This place is a mess. You have to guide me.* The next morning when Paul woke up, God gave him a name. Paul then visited Jim Stauffer, who owned Ames Construction. He told Jim about the mission and that we needed someone to design a roof. Without hesitation Jim offered his services. A couple of months later Paul came back with a whole team, which in one week put the brand-new metal roof on our building.

By this time we had given the responsibility for getting a deed to the property to a Haitian pastor who said he had lots of contacts. He guaranteed that with the help of his lawyer he would get the job done. October came around all too quickly, and we were nowhere near getting the deed. I began to get very nervous. I cried out to God, "You have to do something!" There was only silence. It seemed like God was deaf.

I continued to try to raise funds, as I knew the time was short. I tried to avoid letting people know we had no deed, but it seemed that everywhere I turned people asked about it. The results were bad—no deed, no money.

At the end of November it was obvious there was no way we were going to have a deed, much less have the $90,000. In the first week of December I finally decided to let Terry Nelson know that things were not looking very good at our end. I didn't want to make the call, but I knew I had to. I was still leaning on the fact that if we just had a deed, this would be a done deal. I was trying to justify in my mind that it was not my fault that God hadn't done anything.

Just the month before, an evangelist from Sweden by the name of Gösta Öman had visited us. He was eighty-four years old and had been in South Korea during the Second World War. He told us that after the war there was a great famine in South Korea because the bombs had destroyed all the rice crops. People were literally starving to death. Gösta had left the army and gone back to South Korea with enough money to survive for three years. In one month he had used almost all his money feeding people. There was one young boy in particular he had become very fond of. The boy used to come into his garden each day and sit with him. One day Gösta noticed that the boy hadn't been around for a while. When he asked his gardener where the boy was, the gardener said that the boy had died the night before. Gösta was heartbroken and shocked. He could not believe things had gotten so bad.

"Why didn't you tell me?" Gösta asked. The gardener, ashamed and sad, raised his head, looked into the eyes of his employer and friend, and said, "You have done so much. We know you have nothing left to give." This was true. Gösta was already preparing to leave the country, as he had run out of funds. He replied, "Don't ever do that to me again. If someone comes here hungry and asks for food, you tell them he can be fed."

At that Gösta went straight into the center of the town to the governor's office. Bursting into a meeting, he threw his hat on the table and asked the people present what they were going to do about all the people dying of starvation. They looked up at him sadly and said they had been thinking about what they might be able to do, but they had found no answers.

The Swedish evangelist said, "Send fifty thousand people to me, and I will feed them." The governor gave him a seal as an agreement, calling him "The Man of Fifty Thousand."

Gösta bought one bag of rice, as it was all he could afford, took it home, and told his housekeeper to put it in a bin with these instructions: "Everyone who comes, give him a cup of rice from the bin until it is finished." The very next day people started to come. Hundreds of people grew to thousands. The line was a mile long every day. Six months later, Gösta's housekeeper came to him and told him the bag was finished. Gösta fell to his knees as he realized that God had fed all those people with only one bag of rice. This was truly a miracle.

So I had this man in my house, with his stories of miracle after miracle. As I listened to him, I again thought—*why didn't God heal my mother?* God had told me He wept for her, but I still wanted to know why she wasn't healed. Why hadn't He done a miracle for *me?*

At that time people were saying that I was such a man of faith, going where no one else wanted to go. But I knew that wasn't the case. Everything I did, I did with a backup plan. I had plan A, B, C, and D. I said of the different things we did, "We'll do this through faith. We don't have the finances, but that's okay." Then my hand would touch my wallet to make sure I had my credit card—just in case God dropped me.

I realized that my life was a sham of faith. I appeared to be walking in faith just because I was going places no one else wanted to go. As I looked at all my backups I wondered whether I had ever really trusted God completely.

I asked Gösta to explain his miracles to me. My mind could not understand how you could feed over a mile long of people for six months with only one bag of rice. And no backups.

I finally got the courage to tell this holy man about my mother and my struggle with God because He had not healed her. I asked him what he thought. Looking at me with his smiling, grandfatherly eyes, he said with all seriousness, "Oh, Terry! I understand now. God gave me a vision of you. You were like a big horse. You had leather straps around you that were tied to a cart. But the cart was too heavy for you to pull, and yet you still tried to pull it. As you pulled, the leather straps were stretching, and you could hear them popping. Even your muscles and joints began to pop under the stress of how hard you were trying to pull the cart." He added firmly, "Terry, God would have done it."

Something clicked in me at that moment. I still didn't understand why God hadn't healed my mother, but I knew He was able. Many years ago the wound had formed in me. In DTS God had shown me His heart in the situation, and now He was saying it wasn't a problem with ability. I released the doubt I'd had and was satisfied that God *could have* healed. Faith began to grow in me, taking the place of my doubt. My mother went on to live into her sixties, but she was never completely healed in this life.

All this happened before I made my call to Terry Nelson in December. With renewed hope in God's ability, I called. Terry was irate when I spoke to him. He had been counting on the money, and I wasn't fulfilling my part of the agreement. He was desperately in need of the $90,000. As we talked I reverted to "man's" thinking and said, "You know, Terry, how can you expect me to get $90,000 for a property I don't have the deed for?"

That made him even madder!

"You knew in the beginning there wasn't a deed. You signed the agreement with the understanding that there wasn't a deed."

I knew I had, but the reality was that no one wanted to give money to a property without a deed. That was my problem. Nothing had been resolved, but Terry hadn't yet told us to get off the property.

On Sunday, December 13, I went off to a quiet place to pray. "What is going on? Why aren't You providing the $90,000? Have You brought us to this point only to drop us?" I cried out to God.

I was straining with all my ability to hear something from God. All of a sudden I sensed Him repeating the words I had spoken to Him: "If you ever give me another chance for this property, I will trust You and not man."

It was like a butterfly coming out of a cocoon. I felt like I was being squeezed mentally, but when I finished that afternoon, I had a whole new way of thinking. I realized that I had been saying that without a deed God could not give us the property. Again I had placed the authority of man above the authority of God. Sharon Ambler, one of the team members, had kept saying throughout those seven years, "God has given us a property."

"If God has given us a property, we would be in it," I would snap back.

"One day you'll see, Terry," she always replied.

With the realization that God had given us the property no matter what, I knew that we had to align and repent to accept the gift God had given us.

The next day, December 14, we had a leadership meeting in the morning. It was there that I described what God had taken me through and how I felt that we had to ask for God's forgiveness, and for the forgiveness of Terry Nelson. We also needed to take up an offering as an act of repentance. I phoned our board members to tell them what had happened. I told Fran Paris that we should not worry about the deed anymore because God had given us the property and He would make a way. To my shock and surprise every board member, who had previously been against the deedless property, agreed. I then called our mission partners, who also were in 100 percent agreement.

That night the YWAM base met together. I apologized as a leader, telling them that we should have moved into the property seven years ago, but I had blown it. Here I was still trusting in man, not God. As a result we were again on the verge of losing the property. That night twenty-three Haitian, American, Canadian, and Norwegian YWAMers gave $3,500. Most of it was in IOUs. But the money all came in, and many individuals had miracle stories of how God had provided for them to fulfill their IOUs.

The next day I went to Port-au-Prince with Maula Jean Marie, the current director of YWAM Gonaives. We split up when we arrived so that I could go quickly to Terry Nelson and ask him for his forgiveness. Maula went to file for the paperwork to legalize us and pursue the deed. Even though we were no longer controlled by the deed, we knew it was important to have the property legally recognized.

Terry wasn't happy to see me. While we were talking, his wife called him on the phone. It was obvious she was upset, and Terry passed the phone over to me so that I could talk to her. She began to give me an earful, rightfully so. In tears I asked her for forgiveness. I told her that we were going to do whatever it took until the $90,000 was all paid. At last I was beginning to walk by faith.

Incredibly, both Terry and his wife forgave me. They said that YWAM could have the property and asked us to give as we could. I could not believe it. Not only that, but there seemed to be a real healing between us as leaders. Even today, as a result of this healing, YWAM and Light Ministries work together and pray for each other.

I left Terry with hope in my heart and met up with Maula on the street. I had never seen him so excited. "Terry, I don't know what has happened, but something has happened."

Maula had gone into the office to organize the papers. Until now we'd always met with a closed door, but this time Maula was given the red-carpet treatment. The director himself welcomed him, and within moments had processed all the beginning paper work. "Terry, we are on our way!" Maula laughed.

As we were laughing and talking on the street, a car drove up beside us. In it were Jacques and Gladys Fourcande, whom we had met when we helped at their orphanage in Citi Soleil. They invited us to get into the car with them, and we started telling them what had happened. Jacques and Gladys looked at each other and then at us and said, "Now it makes sense! We were supposed to leave Haiti in November but have been unable to leave. We felt God say we could not go until we helped you, but we didn't know how."

The Fourcandes said they would take care of the deed. By April 1999 we had a legal, tax-free property straight from the government of Haiti. The Fourcandes had done in four months what would usually have taken years, and it had cost us nothing.

Forty-eight hours from the time we had repented and made a covenant with God, we had seen forgiveness for debt, a breakthrough in the government had occurred recognizing us as a mission, and this influential couple had taken the deed off our hands. A week after they handed us our deed, they flew to America. It was miraculous.

The day after Maula and I returned from Port-au-Prince I was checking my e-mail. I had sent a message to a short list of people explaining what was happening. Evidently the message had spread like wildfire. I received an e-mail from a man I didn't know who wrote, "God has told me to give $10,000 to your mission to help with the $90,000 debt." Along with other gifts we were able to give $13,000 to Light Ministries in the first month. In January, February, and March we gave a little over $10,000 each month. Before this time our mission had received in a single year no more that $60,000 in donations. Now we had nearly exceeded that in four months, over and above the cost of our expenditures. In April only $4,000 came in. I prayed and said, "God, I really believe that you want us to give $10,000 again this month. I am asking for $6,000, and I have no idea how You are going to bring it, but surprise me!"

That Sunday a girl from one of our teams was talking in her home church in the United States about what God was doing in Haiti. God spoke to a man in her congregation, telling him to give $6,000 toward our property. It took him two weeks to figure out how to get the money to us. He sent it first to YWAM Tyler, who forwarded it on, but we received the money that month and gave another $10,000 to Light Ministries.

From that time on we have seen an escalation in every area of our ministry. Thousands began to accept Christ through crusades. Partners abroad began to join with us, and staff began to increase. Funds came through our mission, and all we did was pass them on. We asked God to bless us so that we could be a blessing.

# EIGHT

# Prayer, Praise, and Provision

W E  W E R E  so caught up in prayer that we didn't notice the sun begin to rise. As we stood on the front porch of the base, two other YWAMers and I began to sing worship songs to the Lord. Looking over the green grass, the beautiful flowers, and the tall palm trees, we found it was hard to believe that it was only our first year there.

As we worked on the buildings of the base, hungry to see growth and restoration, God started to give us another type of hunger. It started with only a few of us: we became hungry for prayer.

Each morning we met early to pray, and God began to teach us. Our worship and prayer time was not just about singing a few songs. One afternoon, a few weeks into our new prayer time, I was sitting in my office browsing through the books on my shelf. I came across one I had not read in a while, *Could You Not Tarry One Hour* by Larry Lee. Larry had taken the Lord's prayer and used it as an outline for steps of prayer, beginning with praise and then praying for God's kingdom to come, for provision, for forgiveness, and for God's power for the day. I began to realize that this was what we were doing in our prayer time.

Simultaneously our prayer meetings were growing in intensity and authority. As we met each morning, we started to pray in God's will for the city and for our ministry in a way we had never done before.

Our staff began taking steps of faith. Illioney St. Fleur, a Haitian who had done a DTS in 1995, started a mobile team. He took a group of Haitians, formed from the last DTS, through Haiti. Everyone joining the team went home for a month to raise funds. At the end of the month they had raised twelve dollars. In faith the team went anyway, with enough money to get to the first city. When they returned three months later, they had over two hundred dollars from gifts. They had eaten like kings, and everywhere they went they were treated wonderfully. God was moving in powerful ways and being so gracious.

After a couple of weeks of morning prayer, God began to show us strategies for the base and for the city. He also showed us what we needed to do to see His strategies become a reality. We felt that God was leading us to believe for the whole city of St. Marc.

As we worshiped our big God, our vision began to grow. We started praying for God to provide water for our mission. We had only one well on the base at that time, and it was contaminated. We carried on praying, asking for well-drilling technicians, and even a well-drilling rig.

A month later a man named Shae Adams, who had been on an outreach to our base four years before, contacted me by e-mail. He wrote, "Terry, I was sitting at a zoo with my family on the weekend. All of a sudden you came to my mind. Then I looked, and there was a windmill pumping water out of the ground. God told me I am supposed to contact you about getting water. Do you have a need for water?"

This was totally out of the blue. I responded immediately. Shae connected a group of people, and the next thing we knew, geologists, water technicians, and engineers were flying over. A complete survey was made, not only of our property but also of the whole city. God didn't want to just bless us; He wanted to bless the whole city through us. The team gave me an official report of the water and drilling conditions and of the kind of drill rig that would work in St. Marc. They went a step further and got a foundation to donate a drill rig, which they shipped to us at their own expense. They then came back down to teach our

Haitian staff how to operate the rig. As a result there are now over fifty wells throughout the city, all producing fresh, clean water.

We had four additional wells drilled on the base, and our existing well was shocked and sealed to make the water cleaner. When we first came to the base, the water had smelled bad. After the shock treatment, there was no smell. Back then we didn't have any washing machines, and we had only one pump. Now we have four electric pumps and a sewer system that regenerates the water for watering the grass. We are irrigating the whole property.

As well as giving us water, God was giving us strategy to pray for mission partners. We realized we were just naive YWAMers. We had spent our whole lives trying to break into the Haitian culture, and we had no idea how to cope with the logistics of running a sophisticated ministry. We began to ask God for people who would be able to help the mission from a professional point of view. We asked for partners from the business sectors of society who could help us bless the people of Haiti in different areas. Paul Martin, who had helped fixed our roof, was the first, but there were more to come.

In another prayer time, while praying for more laborers to Haiti, we had a revelation that if God brought more people, we would need a vehicle to transport them in. We started praying for a bus. "God, we ask you for a bus—not an old bus, but a new bus, and one with air conditioning! We need this bus to accomplish all the things You have called us to do," we prayed.

A few months later I was in the Untied States on a trip. After a time of speaking about what God was doing in Haiti, a businessman came up to me and asked if I would have coffee with him the next morning.

"Is six o'clock too early for you?" he asked.

"That's fine," I laughed.

We met at a small coffee shop inside an antique store. We got our coffee at the counter and sat down at one of the three tables. The man pulled out his wallet from his jacket. He took out a business card and wrote something on the back. I thought, *Oh, good, he's going to give me his personal number.* As he slid the business card over to me faceup, he said, "God has spoken to me to do something. On the back of that card is an amount of money. It should be plenty to buy a new bus. Any extra money I want to go toward other expenses."

I flipped the card over and took a deep breath. On it, he had written $50,000.

The man got the money to me the next day. I expressed it to our bank, and a staff member, Matt Adams, picked out a bus from a dealership in Port-au-Prince. The bus has blessed many people and has increased many people's faith. It has enabled us to bring teams in with confidence. As a result of this gift, we began to average three hundred people a year coming on short-term missions trips under normal circumstances, depending on the situation in the country. The bus can seat twenty-eight passengers and has air conditioning. Other organizations have used it, and we have taken missions teams over to the Dominican Republic in it. Tools and generators also came in—God provided the best of the best.

The next building we started to construct on the base was a 7,500-square-foot duplex at the back of the property. It was to house the two largest families on the base: my own and the Shipleys. As we prayed, the finances came in.

"Ask me anything, and I will give it." God spoke this to my heart one morning as we were praying, and I told the others about it. Strangely we were stumped and didn't really know what to pray, so we tried to pray things that we thought were wise and holy. After the meeting, a few of the team members were talking outside. Naomi Mosley, a young woman on staff at the time, asked, "Terry, why didn't we pray for a swimming pool?" I laughed as if she had told a joke and thought to myself, *Yeah, right, pray for a swimming pool—we have to pay off the duplex first, and we have many other building projects. A swimming pool would be ridiculous to ask for. Who ever heard of missionaries asking for a swimming pool?* God must have been laughing at me. He knew what was to come.

I was scheduled to go on a trip to the United States again. This time I went to Texas and stopped by the YWAM base. I also visited a local church I knew and was able to get an appointment with the missions pastor. I asked if the church would consider helping us with finances to finish the duplex. Half listening, the pastor looked out the window and said wistfully, "I think it is sad that missionaries don't get more time to be refreshed."

*Where did that come from?* I thought, but I went with it. "Yes, that is why we need a duplex so we can have adequate housing. If we could just have adequate housing, that alone would be refreshing." I could see that the missions pastor was still thinking about his first comment.

"It's just not right. Missionaries are giving their all 24/7, laying down their lives."

Cautiously I said, "Yeah." I still wasn't sure where he was going with this, and I wanted to get back to talking about the duplex.

Eventually I could tell that this man was determined to talk about the need for refreshment for missionaries, so I jokingly told him what Naomi had said about the swimming pool before I left. "Can you imagine me ever asking for money for that! It would never happen. No one thinks about missionaries needing to be refreshed."

The missions pastor agreed and said, "If someone was to stand up in my church on Sunday morning and say, 'I want to praise God because He has given me the funds to build a swimming pool in my backyard,' we would all praise God and be encouraged. We wouldn't think twice about it. But if missionaries said they needed a swimming pool to refresh themselves in Haiti, they would have tomatoes thrown at them!"

Our time together had run out, and I left, thinking nothing more about it. A week or so later, while I was still in Texas, I got a call from a member of the pastor's church. "I was talking to our missions pastor, and he happened to bring up the conversation you and he had," he said.

"About the duplex?" I asked.

"No, he was talking about a swimming pool. It isn't right that we don't give our missionaries opportunities to be refreshed. I want to talk to you about having a swimming pool built in YWAM St. Marc."

The man asked me to check into how much it would cost to build a swimming pool. That same day, asking God to guide me, I picked up the yellow pages. The first man I called turned out to be a Christian. I told him who I was, what I was doing, and why I was doing it. He was amazed, saying, "I thought God could never use me, being a swimming pool guy, in the mission field. I will definitely help you with your pool."

We met for breakfast the following day, and the man even paid for my meal. He showed me how to build a swimming pool and came up with a list of materials, suggesting we build a restroom as well. He offered to sell us the materials at cost. I went back to the man from the church. He agreed to pay for it all, as well as a year's supply of chemicals. Everything was shipped to us within a month.

Just a few weeks after I returned to Haiti, the next mission partner to join the group arrived. Paul Martin had arranged another team to come in to help finish the duplex. One of the men he brought in was a wild, middle-aged man from Lancaster, Pennsylvania, named Glenn Weaver. Glenn was a plumber and an electrician and owned a business called Lanco Mechanical. Paul spoke very highly of him and his fast work. "If you tell him to do something, he burns rubber getting it done," he said.

When I met Glenn, he seemed quiet and reserved. Since he was a plumber, I asked him to help us with the swimming pool. I could tell he was shocked that I asked. Later on Paul told me that I needed to explain to the team how God had provided the pool and that it wasn't just my own extravagance.

When Glenn heard the story, he was amazed. The next day he began flying through the base, fixing plumbing problems that had been taking us years to figure out. He arranged the plumbing for the duplex, and he helped us with the swimming pool. After that he was hooked and joined our partners group.

We needed additional resident housing, and we built two units of 20 by 120 feet, with four apartments in each. We called each unit a quadplex. But there was a problem with the interior walls. We had built everything else, and the masonry, which had been done by locals, was complete. A team was coming in, and we needed to finish the apartments in two weeks' time. Paul went back to prayer, and we continued to pray here, "Lord, bring in Your people."

Paul felt that he should telephone Weaver's Construction, owned by Mel Weaver, another wonderful man who loved God with all his heart. Mel came up with an idea for walls that would pop into place. The walls were very light but also sound-resistant. We had all the materials shipped in and had installed them within the two weeks.

Mel came with his wife, Vera-May, to help see the walls installed. At that time Vera-May had a chronic problem with migraines. When she got a migraine, it hit her so hard she had to go immediately to the ER and was usually hospitalized for a couple of days. I knew nothing about this. Mel came to me on the first evening while I was on the porch talking to Glenn and Paul. He said, "We need to pray. Vera-May is coming down with a migraine."

I didn't know how to read Mel very well at that time and just thought, *Okay, it's a headache. Big deal. Take some aspirin. See you in the morning.*

Mel then explained how serious it was.

We gathered around and prayed for Vera-May. Mel went back upstairs. Vera-May had gone to sleep. When she woke up the next morning, the headache was gone. She had been totally healed. Mel was rejoicing, and that morning God began to give him vision for the base. Mel later joined our partners team as the third member. To this day Vera-May has not suffered from another migraine.

God was building and blessing YWAM Haiti both spiritually and physically.

During those years we saw God use prayer to release His strategies to bring about His blessings.

# NINE

# Possessing the Land

N E X T to our property was an old rum factory. As I drove past it one blazing hot day, in my heart I suddenly felt God say, "This land is yours, too." The thought came out of nowhere, but by this time I recognized God's voice. I thanked Him and prayed that He would show me how to obtain it.

A short time later a Haitian woman who was living in New York turned up on our doorstep. She said the rum-factory property was hers, and she offered to sell it to us. I was amazed. We hadn't told anyone we wanted to buy the property. I felt this must be God.

The woman said that the land was an inheritance from her father. She explained too that her brother, a local gang leader named Freole, was trying to sell the property himself and take the money. Freole was addicted to drugs and a dangerous man. He had begun to sell other property belonging to his sister around the city.

As the woman sat in my office, I asked what kind of price she wanted. She said she would need $170,000 for the 1.3 acres of land.

Internally I gasped. "Well, let's talk," I said.

I took the woman for a walk around the base and told her of our vision and heart for the people of Haiti and how we wanted to help them. "If you give us this property, it will be used to bless the people of Haiti," I said.

The woman was visibly touched and almost instantaneously agreed to lower the asking price to our suggested sum of $60,000. We felt we should go ahead because of what God had already spoken to us. However, the woman wanted the money right away.

"There is no way we can give it all now. We need to do some investigation on the property and have some time to get the money," I said.

Eventually she agreed and gave us four weeks to find the money.

Lubens Romulus, a Haitian staff member, arranged to go to the notary with her and her relatives to sign the buyer's contract. We would need to put $1,000 down as a deposit. This was all the money we had in the bank.

When Freole heard that we were intending to buy the land, he started to cause a lot of trouble. He began to threaten both his sister and our mission. He screamed at us from the gate, "If you buy this land, we will kill you. You will be cursed."

Despite Freole's threats, we arrived at the notary's office to sign the contract for the property. As we arrived, we could see Freole's gang members starting to appear. They surrounded the notary's office, flashing their guns and trying to intimidate us. I could see that Freole's sister was very jumpy. I wanted to get the whole thing over with as quickly as possible.

The notary was a man of about seventy years of age. He could barely see. He seemed to have no idea of the situation that was brewing outside. Slowly he walked around the room to the shelves of dusty books. There were no computers; all of the land transactions were in paper form piled high around the room. Slowly the notary drew up the contract. While he was writing, one of the gang members suddenly banged his gun against the metal door. The noise made us all jump. We looked anxiously at the door, praying that the men wouldn't start shooting at us.

The notary looked up at me and smiled. "Don't worry about them!" he said. I was glad *he* was so relaxed.

Since the house had no electricity, the notary opened the windows of his office to give himself more light to see the contract. I was sure that in a second a shot would fire into the house. The notary's assistant, another old man, found the right book to make the entry. The transaction seemed to be taking forever. The two old men decided that there still wasn't enough light and called us all outside into the backyard among the squawking chickens and washing. The smell of urine was strong in the air.

Eventually the notary showed us what we needed to sign. The gang members were still glaring at us. It looked like there was going to be an Old-West shoot-out before the day was done.

Cautiously I sat on a very unstable-looking chair to sign the contract. When it was all finished, and we couldn't linger any longer in the relative safety of the office, Lubens and I were the first to step outside, praying fervently under our breath. I didn't know what was going to happen. However, instead of the carnage that I had imagined, nothing happened. We walked quickly to our cars and left. The gang didn't touch us. Freole's sister got on the first plane back to New York.

That evening I rejoiced, thinking it was all over. I sent an e-mail telling our supporters the story of the property. In three weeks' time, $65,000 had come in. God had provided over and above what we needed.

Freole didn't give up so easily. He had threatened his sister with a gun before she got on the plane, and his gang started to surround us and threaten every Haitian member of the mission. They followed and tried to intimidate me wherever I went.

Some of our staff nearly left the mission because they were so terrified. We had to have times of prayer dealing with fear, continually asking God to confirm His Word to those who were afraid. One staff member came to me after a particularly difficult night.

"God doesn't want us to lose our lives over land," she said.

"If He has told us that the land is ours, we have to claim it," I replied. "We need to possess the land and not bow down to fear."

As a base we made the decision not to let fear control our lives. Only the Word of God would control us. I felt that more was at stake than just the rum-factory land. If we did not follow through with this property, we would lose the property we were in as well. People in the city would know that we could be intimidated.

Haiti is a nation dedicated to voodoo, essentially a fear-based religion. If you do not allow fear to dictate, 90 percent of the battle is won. Curses cannot attach themselves without a spirit of fear. Learning this nullifies the works of Satan, and the effect of voodoo is dissolved.

We stuck to our decision to buy the land. But Freole's gang continued to threaten and intimidate, telling us we were all going to die. Freole particularly liked to shout over our wall the different ways we would die. Every night his gang would show up on the rum-factory property performing voodoo ceremonies, shouting, and cursing. They would rake their machetes across the outer wall of our property. The noise was terrible. A YWAM team from Jamaica was staying with us at the time. They would stay up all night praying for our safety and protection. No one could get any sleep, because starting at midnight, Freole would yell, scream, and shoot for a couple of hours. The gang had intimidated the police and neighborhood so much that nobody would go near them, let alone arrest them.

This was a challenging time for all of us. We had to trust God for our lives. We were going into a whole new level of spiritual warfare.

We made it through the four weeks, and the time came to pay the rest of the money for the property. The intimidation intensified. It became clear that Freole had stolen from other relatives. His corruption was being exposed through our one purchase. Another notary had falsely made up papers, and a judge had been paid off to allow the other purchases. So far Freole had gotten away with it, but not anymore.

We had one final survey on the land before the money was to be exchanged. The police came to watch over the proceedings, but the surveyor didn't want to come, because he had received threats. But finally he arrived, everything was done, and we paid the money. The property was ours. I breathed a sigh of relief. (There was still a wall between the old rum-factory land and the rest of our base. The new land was empty apart from a small mud hut with a tin roof where a guardian and his family stayed.)

A few days later Lubens, Brian, and I stood on the second floor of the unfinished duplex, looking over at our new land. Suddenly I saw

Freole and his gang entering the property. Freole started fighting with another gang member. Dust flew as they began punching each other and rolling around on the ground.

We ran from the duplex and down the road to the entrance of the new land. Just as we got there, one of the gang members came flying out of the front gate, straight across the road. He slammed into a door and knocked it down as he tried to escape Freole, who was right behind him. The two men ran through the tiny passages between the shacks. All we could hear was banging and crashing as they ran into walls, past chickens and goats. Finally, on unsteady feet, Freole came out, dirty and with blood on his hands. He walked back onto our land with a look of scorn, as if to say, "You dare try to stop me."

"What are we going to do? We can't let him get away with this. He is on our land," I said, looking at the others.

As we walked toward the land, another gang member, named Ti Blac, came out to the front. Shaking with anger he screamed at us, "This is our land, and nobody is going to have it unless we allow it."

We later found out that Freole and the first gang member had gotten into a fight because Freole hadn't paid him for staying up all those nights and intimidating us. Freole had promised him a portion of the land in exchange for working for him. Now Freole had no land to give.

"We can't allow this," I said, looking over at Brian and Lubens.

All three of us began to walk onto the new property. Ti Blac started walking backwards, still shouting, "Nobody can have the land unless we allow it." As we walked toward him, his voice became less and less confident.

"We'll never have this land secure if we allow him to get away with this," I said to the others. But we didn't know what to do. As we were walking, for some reason I started waving my arms as if shooing chickens out of the way.

"Get out of here, get out of here," I shouted.

Sheepishly Ti Blac bowed his head, and to my amazement he walked away. Lubens, Brian, and I looked at one another in surprise. I could only put it down to the authority of God.

As we continued walking farther onto the property, we realized that Freole had hidden himself behind the guardian's house. He had only one way out. I knew it was a dangerous situation. If you run a wild boar to a cliff where it can't escape, it'll run you down. I was expecting Freole to charge any minute.

By this time the whole neighborhood was watching what was going on. It appeared that the showdown had finally come.

"God, what do we do? We need Your help," we quietly prayed.

Suddenly Freole came storming out. He reminded me of the demon-possessed man in the Bible with many legions of demons in him. He was foaming at the mouth, dirt all over him, eyes glowing. He ran straight up to me and stopped inches from my face. I didn't know how I was able to stay still. I glanced behind me and could see that Brian and Lubens were right there. All I could think of was the scripture in Ephesians 6:13: "Therefore put on the full armor of God, so that when the day of evil comes, you may be able to stand your ground, and after you have done everything, to stand."

I stood. I didn't move a muscle. Having backed away, Freole came all the way up to me again and starting cursing, acting like he was about to spit on me. This was too much for me. I said to God, "You know I love You, You know I want to be a good Christian. But I'm also a Texan. If he spits on me, I don't know what I'm going to do."

Freole tried to spit. But his mouth was dry and foaming like a mad dog, and only drool fell onto his own shirt. He tried to brush it away, as if it hadn't really happened. As he tried to spit again, I looked straight at him.

"You better not spit on me," I said.

In reply he looked down at my shoes. I couldn't believe it! In Texas it was a huge insult to spit on a person's shoes. Freole aimed at my shoes and spat. Five little pellets hit the dust around my foot. Not one drop hit my shoes. I continued to stand my ground.

"You killed my father!" he suddenly shouted.

"What!" I exclaimed. I had never met his father, but I knew that his father had been shot four times in the head on that very land a couple of years before we moved next door.

I continued trying to listen to God. All of a sudden He began to give me insight into things to say. God gave me confidence, and as it increased, Freole's confidence seemed to diminish.

"I don't know who killed your father, but I do know someone who does," I said.

Freole's eyes grew really big.

"I could tell you about my father," he shouted.

"Well, why don't you tell me about your father. I'd like to hear about him," I replied as calmly as I could.

All of a sudden he started crying and walking away from the property. Through his tears he whimpered, "I could tell you about my father! I could tell you about my father!" The whole neighborhood was watching him cry. Since most of the Haitians couldn't speak English, they didn't understand what was going on. They just watched open-mouthed at the transformation of the feared Freole. This gang leader was the one who was now afraid. We had just seen the authority of God in action.

As Freole walked off the land, everybody began to laugh, shouting, "Terry beat Freole!" That night and the whole next day people were shouting, "The God of Terry is greater than the god of Freole!" Even the guardian on the property, who had been hired by Freole, was heard by some of the YWAM staff singing praises. He was making up his own song of the story, singing to his family how the God of Terry had conquered the god of Freole and his voodoo and all his gang.

After that we never saw Freole on the property again. A few years later I bumped into him. The transformed man said, "Terry, not only is this city yours, but this country is yours too. You should run for president!"

God had taught us a new lesson with the rum-factory land. We had to claim the property. God brought the provision quickly, but we had to physically claim the land. Fear could not control us; only the Word of God could.

We had an official dedication of the property in January 2000, giving it over for the purposes of God. After that we held a crusade. I preached on how God wants to bless and not curse Haiti and how we need to turn from our sins. At the end of the message, I asked people at the meeting to dedicate the land to God. I knelt down with seven hundred Haitians. As a community we all prayed, "This land is God's. It will not be stolen or used for things not of God. We give it for the purposes of God to be a blessing to the city."

About this time many people had been questioning Ingvild and me, asking us if it was right for us to raise our five children in Haiti. We knew that God had called us as a family to Haiti, but we had to learn to trust God for our children's safety. Once, when Ingvild had been dealing with anxiety over this issue, God had given her a promise. He said that if she entrusted our children to Him, He would take care of them in Haiti and she would not have to worry. From then on Ingvild had complete peace.

This promise had been put to the test in 1998. Ingvild was looking after the children alone. I had just left with Brian Shipley to drive to the Dominican Republic to meet Loren Cunningham, the founder of YWAM. We were bringing Loren back to Haiti to visit our base. We arrived at the Santo Domingo YWAM center around five o'clock in the evening and were greeted by Kent Norrell, the YWAM director.

"Take a seat, Terry, I have some bad news for you," Kent said.

I sat down, my mind racing, wondering what had happened. Kent explained that my son Wayne, then aged nine, had fallen off his bicycle and broken his elbow. I breathed a sigh of relief. No one had died, and a broken elbow wasn't too serious, I thought. I was wrong. Evidently the break was bad. The doctors couldn't find a pulse in the arm, and they were worried it would need to be amputated.

In a panic I tried to get ahold of Ingvild, but I couldn't get through. A few hours later I received some good news. Wayne had been able to get to a U.S. naval hospital in Port-au-Prince. The U.S. Navy was in Haiti as part of the UN peacekeeping force. When Wayne arrived at the hospital, it just so happened an orthopedic surgeon had been flown in from America for three weeks. Wayne went into surgery that evening. Pins were put into his elbow, and a pulse was found, which meant his arm was saved!

The navy doctors asked Ingvild and Wayne to fly over to the United States to take him to a proper hospital and make sure that the arm really was okay. My wife and son took the next flight to Miami, and I met them there. Sharon Ambler was in the United States at the time and was able to get us straight into a children's hospital. We had no insurance, but amazingly the hospital didn't charge us. When the specialist looked at the X-rays, he said he had never seen such a good job. He said he couldn't have done better himself. We were free to go home.

At the end of it all, the orthopedic surgeon from the U.S. Navy wrote to us saying he was a Christian. He said he had felt God say that the reason He had sent him to Haiti was to help Wayne. God had fulfilled His promise. Wayne was looked after better than we could have asked or imagined. His arm healed perfectly, with no complications.

A few years after this incident, Ingvild gave birth to Ethan-Paul, our fifth child. We didn't want to go to the local hospital, as it was not sanitary and had no equipment. Wayne had been born at a hospital in the United States in 1989. Kristian was born in 1990 with the help of a midwife on the YWAM Tyler base. Elizabeth was born in Haiti in 1992 on an army cot, which was more rustic than a home birth. And Samuel was born in 1994 in our home in Haiti. We decided we wanted another home birth.

I arranged for three doctors to be on hand for the birth. If one was gone, two others would be there. If two were gone, at least one would be there to help with the birth. All of our children had been born late, two weeks after their due date. We told the doctors this, and Ingvild had all the necessary examinations. The baby was due in February 2000. To our shock, two weeks early, Ethan-Paul decided it was time to come out.

It was early morning. Ingvild woke up about four o'clock to go to the bathroom. Suddenly her water broke. I was still sleeping. Ingvild woke me up a couple of hours later to tell me that the baby was on its way.

*Great, we finally have one coming early!* I thought.

After a quick cup of coffee, I jumped into the car and went to the first doctor. He wasn't there, so I went to the second doctor. I met him as he was coming out the door of his office with his suitcase on his way to Miami.

"I'll be back next week," he said.

"My wife is giving birth now! She can't wait till next week," I replied in desperation.

With growing panic I sped over to the last doctor. He wasn't available either. All three doctors were unavailable. I began to get concerned. I went back to tell Ingvild the bad news.

As I got home I suddenly remembered that Cheryl Shipley had a book entitled *Where There Is No Doctor*. With the help of the book, perhaps we could deliver the baby ourselves, I thought to myself. I went upstairs to check on Ingvild, who was very relaxed and peaceful. Since she had already given birth four times, this was nothing new to her. I called Cheryl, who had four children of her own and had some experience working as a nurse in the United States. After discussing the situation with Cheryl, she said she thought she could deliver the baby. Ingvild felt peace about the decision, so we went ahead.

About six o'clock that night the contractions got serious. All of the YWAM staff were downstairs, and Ingvild was upstairs in our bedroom, which thankfully had air-conditioning.

"Terry, you have to help me," Ingvild said, now with tension in her voice.

Cheryl was there with her book open at the right page, ready to start. Suddenly I remembered something.

"When two of the other four children were born, their umbilical cords were wrapped around their necks. They were nearly choked. If we see the same thing on this baby, we have to get the cord off quickly, or the baby could be strangled," I said to Cheryl in a panic.

Suddenly it was time for Ingvild to push. Everything was quiet. Cheryl was at the foot of the bed, one eye on the baby coming and one eye on the book. Before too long I saw the top of the baby's head as I crouched down behind Cheryl. Sweating from nerves I began thinking I should have looked harder for another doctor.

All of a sudden Ingvild gave a good push, and the baby's head came out. As I looked I saw the cord wrapped around the baby's head. I shouted at Cheryl, pointing to the head.

"Cord! Cord!" I screamed.

"I see it, I see it," she replied, calmly flipping the cord around and off the neck. I thought all was well until I realized that the baby wasn't coming out anymore. Ingvild was just lying on the bed, exhausted, with her eyes closed. I felt something was wrong. Images flashed through my mind of picking up my wife halfway through giving birth and taking her to the hospital, which had no emergency room or beds.

Quietly Ingvild asked, "Should I push?"

Cheryl and I both shouted, "Yes!" And with a whoosh Ethan-Paul Quentin Snow was born.

Cheryl quickly put the syringe in the baby's mouth and sucked out all the fluid. As she did this, Ethan-Paul let out a scream, and I laughed with relief. Cheryl had done an amazing job.

I went downstairs to tell everyone. In my excitement I phoned Paul Martin. It was in Paul's house that we had found out that Ingvild was pregnant. We were not planning on having any more children and had been very content with four, but it was a nice surprise. The day we found out that Ingvild was pregnant, Paul and his wife, Judy, took us shopping. They bought us a brand-new, top-of-the-line washer and dryer. This was a very timely gift, since our very old washer had totally worn out. We hadn't known what we were going to do.

We decided we wanted to name our child after Paul, as he had made such an impact on our lives and our mission. He helped us go to a whole new level in believing God for the impossible. We wanted Ethan-Paul to have the same kind of characteristics.

Once again God was faithful to us, honoring his promises. Over and over again we saw His hand caring for our children in different ways. With our new family of five, we moved into the duplex on the base, excited about the future. Our family was complete at seven, but God hadn't stopped yet with the expansion of the base.

# TEN

# Out into the Community

BRIAN SHIPLEY had driven Loren Cunningham over to Haiti while I had been in the United States looking after Wayne and his broken elbow. When I returned to Haiti a few days later, I walked around the base with Loren, describing our vision to him. As we walked through the grounds, Loren turned to me and said, "You know what, Terry, big vision eats up lots of property." He pointed to some empty land to the right side of our property, asking who owned it and whether it was possible to buy it. I told him that the owners actually had contacted us and asked if we were interested in buying, but we had said no. We didn't think we needed any more land. With a knowing smile Loren again said, "Big vision eats up lots of property."

I got the message, and over the next couple of years prayed about the land. As I prayed I felt God say that He wanted us to have it. He was telling us to expand our borders.

In the summer of 2000 the owner of the land Loren had pointed to came back to us, asking if we would like to buy the property. This time I said yes, and we started to negotiate a price.

The owner offered the land to us for $600,000. This amount seemed extortionate, but the owner explained that if he sold the land in small lots, that would be the total price he could get. As he liked our mission and what we were doing, he said he wanted to sell the land to us. Paul Martin flew in to help us. As a retired businessman, he gave invaluable help and advice. We ended up bartering with the owner, and by a miracle the price came down to $181,000, less than a quarter of the original asking price. We agreed to buy the property for that amount and signed an agreement stating that we would pay it in a few months. Buying the land would double the size of our base to eight acres.

As soon as the agreement was signed, the spiritual attack started again. We had been running soccer tournaments on the base because there was a need in the community and we had the space to be able to put on a tournament. We wanted to use the event as a means of discipling the community by using biblical values as the rules of conduct. We encouraged the players to be good sportsmen. Often, if a team lost in Haiti, machetes would be pulled out and rioting and fighting would take place. Police would be paid off to turn a blind eye.

In 1998 the zone had put on the tournament themselves, and it was a disaster. The next year we organized the event, and it was a huge success. Everyone in St. Marc raved about it because there was no violence. When I went into government offices, people stopped what they were doing to say hello.

"This is Terry Snow from Jeunesse en Mission who hosted the soccer tournament," they would say.

From our small effort to serve and bless the city, we were given fame and favor.

At the very first tournament, we decided we would open in prayer. It was a simple prayer: "God bless the teams. May no one get hurt." All the people from the community responded by standing up and applauding. They were not Christians. They applauded because praying was so new and they liked the novelty.

When we signed the agreement to buy the third property, we were in the second year of running the tournament. Soccer teams were leaving other championship tournaments in the city just to participate in our tournament because it was so well organized and our trophies were so nice. The matches were televised and broadcast by radio. Lubens Romulus was doing a fantastic job of organizing everything.

At this time we still had a wall up between our base and the new land. The property had a sharecrop plan that grew tomatoes and bananas. I had just returned from a speaking engagement in Morehead City, North Carolina, and was getting briefed on how things were going on the base. The tournament was going well, but a man was trying to sell beer over the wall from the sharecrop land that we were in the process of buying. Lubens had asked him not to do it, but the man would not listen. Officially we were responsible for the land, since we had signed the contract of sale.

The beer seller was reaching over, passing beer bottles to the crowd. I went over and told him he couldn't sell there. As I was walking over, I felt an impression from God that once we did this we were going to go into a whole new level of spiritual warfare.

The seller started yelling at me. I told him that he was on our property, but he screamed back that it was his land. It was obvious that he was unaware of our purchase agreement. Lubens and I realized that we had to go over to the other side of the wall to get the guy to stop.

To be on the safe side, we took some security men from the soccer championship with us. It was normal to have security around at matches to help oversee ticket sales and any problems that might occur. As we reached the beer seller, he went berserk. I went over to move his table, all the while telling him he was on our land and had to get off it. Suddenly he charged at me with anger in his eyes. Two of the security men stepped in front of me to block him and grabbed him by his arms. The man was still screaming at me, telling me the land was his and he could do what he liked.

All of a sudden Lubens whispered to me, indicating gang members from the neighborhood who were appearing from the bushes here and there. I knew we needed to get out of there. We left quickly, hoping we had made our point. About thirty minutes later I saw a woman in the same spot as the man, selling beer over the wall. The original beer seller was beating down a post that held up the barbed wire along the wall so that he could pass beer through more easily. He had also made a hole in the wall to pass beer through.

As one of the bottles was being passed through, it was dropped, and broken glass and beer went everywhere. Exasperated, I again went over to the other side of the wall. When the woman saw me, she became very angry. She had an ice pick in her hand and was holding it up like a weapon. I was trapped. I felt that as soon as I turned my back she was going to stab me. I wrestled the pick out of her hands and threw it into the brush.

"You can't sell beer here anymore," I told her.

As I was saying this I noticed the gang men appearing again. They looked hostile, and I knew I had to get out of there.

Lubens and I went back to the soccer match. It didn't appear that we had any more problems. Lubens advised me to file a complaint with the police so that they would be aware of what had happened. This is normal legal procedure for Haiti. But by the time the tournament had finished for the day, the reporting office was closed. We agreed to go the next morning.

That night a huge thunderstorm flooded the soccer field. We had to drain the field or the tournament would be cancelled. We got the pumps out. It was hard work, but eventually the field was drained. But then the generator needed an oil change. I serviced it so it would be ready for that evening. We planned to go to the police station as soon as I was finished. At about noon Lubens was on his way to get cleaned up from drying out the field when a police truck turned up at the gate. The police started calling for Lubens. I didn't think much of it, because I knew Lubens had a lot of friends on the police force.

Eventually I realized that the police were upset, so I went over to see what was going on. As I walked outside, wiping the oil off my hands with a cloth, a policeman said, "There's Terry. Take him." The police showed me a paper telling me to come to court immediately. Since Lubens was barefoot, the police let him go get his shoes. Lubens knew that they were giving him a chance to escape. I got ahold of a few staff members and instructed some of them to follow us to wherever we were taken.

When we got to the courthouse, I found out what was going on. The beer seller had filed a legal charge against us declaring that we had attacked him and broken all of his beer bottles. He also claimed that

Lubens and I had gone to his house during the night and smashed it up. I assumed that the matter wouldn't take long, as it was obvious that the man was just looking for money and that his charges were outrageous.

But the case kept going and going. The judge kept dragging it out. As the beer seller started to tell his side of the story, a lawyer whom we called on from time to time showed up. He had been passing by and had heard that we were inside and so he had come in. He listened to the beer seller's story, and then he heard our story. He proceeded to rip the beer seller's story apart. By the time he was done, the land that the beer seller called his was brought into question. The man had no proof of ownership, and I had the paper from the agreement of sale. The charge of breaking into his house was dropped because again he couldn't prove anything, but the charge of attacking him was upheld.

"Why would Terry attack you?" our lawyer asked.

The man didn't know what to say and took counsel from several of his friends.

Eventually he said, "Because he could." He claimed I beat him up because I liked beating people up. Finally after cross-examination, his story changed. He said I had slapped him and Lubens had pushed him.

"My goodness, we are going to have to arrest all of St. Marc for pushing and slapping. That happens on a daily basis," the lawyer said, laughing. He asked immediately for the justice of the peace to throw the case out, but the justice refused.

The judge asked me more questions. As I was explaining things to him again, he received a letter. Later on I found out the letter was from the second commissaire du gouvernement. (There are three commissaires du gouvernement in each city, labeled one, two, and three. The role of the commissaire is to organize and verify trial dates. Commissaires are more important than the justice of the peace and are appointed by the government.) The letter was an order for me to go to prison before I had even finished my testimony. The commissaire in question later claimed that gang members had turned up at his home and told him to sign a paper on his own letterhead without even letting him read it. At first he refused. But when they threatened to burn his house and his family, he gave in.

The justice ordered Lubens and me to jail at the police station. This would mean that we would have to see the commissaire the next day and have our case dealt with. However, Commissaire Frenot overruled and ordered us to go straight to prison. This meant that we would not be dealt with right away and could be kept in prison for an indefinite length of time.

# ELEVEN

# Light in Dark Places

I STILL had the base walkie-talkie and cell phone on me, so I could contact people to let them know what was going on. No one could believe it when I told them I was on my way to prison. I said goodbye to Ingvild over the radio, telling her I loved her. She asked if I was going to be all right. I couldn't answer. It was obvious to us all that this was a setup. I had no idea once I went into prison what I was going to be facing, but I was thankful that Lubens was with me.

The prison guards told us to remove our shoelaces and belts. Then they started talking among themselves about whether they needed to put Lubens and me in separate cells. I pleaded with them to put us together, and thankfully they agreed.

We were put into a fourteen-by-sixteen-foot cell with fourteen other male prisoners and only one small window. There were ten cells altogether, one for the women and nine for the men, with one hundred prisoners altogether. As the guards opened the cell door for Lubens and me, we had to squeeze in; there was hardly a place to stand. Immediately the other prisoners started shouting at us not to step on their sheets and mattresses, forcing us to stay squashed by the doorway. Our only option was to lean against the cement cell wall. I could see that we needed to break the ice with the other prisoners.

"So, who here is guilty of a crime?" I said, laughing nervously.

No one laughed. As I was thinking of something else to say, one man spoke up.

"If you are in a Haitian prison, you are guilty," he said. He meant that you are guilty unless you can prove yourself innocent, unlike other countries where you are innocent until proven guilty.

With that ominous opening we began to tell the other prisoners what had happened to us. One of them offered to share his section and sheets. He told everyone to move over, and the men made a place for us. We took our shoes off at the door and lay in our underwear because it was so hot. The smell was almost unbearable. There were two urine buckets, one by the door and one by the far corner of the cell. The prisoners were very firm with us that these were for urine only. If we needed to do more, we had to wait till the next morning when the guards would let us out. We could tell by the stains on the walls that some people didn't make it. The other prisoners were very concerned that we might not make it, so they kept asking us if we were okay and, if not, we should ask the guard to let us out before they locked us in for the night.

Darkness set in, and the prison became quiet apart from the noise of doors opening and closing. We could hear voices of YWAM staff outside. Apparently a different commissaire du gouvernement had turned up to assist us. As he arrived, the phone rang. We were told later that the prison guard had answered the phone and handed it to the commissaire, who, after speaking, had put the phone down and said that his hands were tied and that he could not help us. We don't know who the phone call was from. It was obvious now that they were trying to make this into a bigger case than it was.

Back at the base the staff had gathered to pray. Ingvild had received a word from God, saying that the way we handled what was happening and the outcome of the situation would determine the future of the mission. Ingvild knew that she had to stay in tune with God and have each step guided clearly by Him. The staff prayed to this end.

I didn't sleep all night. At first there was no electricity, no fan, and no moving air, just a stifling hot cell with a tin roof. We lay like sardines shoulder to feet, packed tightly in the cell, and sweated. I kept wondering what was going to happen. To my amazement Lubens fell straight to sleep. Incredulously I woke him up and asked him how he could sleep in such a situation.

"There's nothing we can do. We might as well sleep," he calmly replied.

I was struggling. I cried out to God, asking him what He was doing. But there was no answer.

At about midnight the electricity came on. The 100-watt bulb right above our heads shined brightly for the rest of the night.

At daybreak people started rustling and getting up. One prisoner folded up his sheet, put it over on one side, then refolded it and put it over to the other side, then kept repeating the ritual. I assumed he was going mad, and I wasn't surprised. The prison was a depressing place.

One prisoner in the cell was called Carrefour, which in Creole means intersection. I watched him stand at the door. Another prisoner saw me looking at him and warned, "Don't go near the door—Carrefour is there. If you go near, he'll hit you."

I was surprised, since Carrefour looked peaceful gazing outside, one hand resting lightly on the bars. But then I saw his fist, tightly clenched as if ready to hit something. The others said he was crazy and was in prison for fighting.

After a little while the guards let us outside to bathe. We were each given a gallon jug of water and told to wash ourselves. The outhouse we had to use stank to high heaven.

Rats were all over it. We heard them scurrying away as we came out of the cell. The only toilet paper available was the used paper plates that the guards had eaten from.

Lubens and I washed our faces, and after ten minutes the guards ushered us all back to the cell. I spoke to the guard and asked if I could sit outside for a while so I could collect my thoughts in the fresh air. A few of the guards standing near said that that would be fine; I wasn't going anywhere. However, one guard refused. He said we had to follow procedure and I had to stay locked up. Disappointed I went back to the cell. According to my watch, it was only seven o'clock. It felt like at least ten o'clock. This was going to be a long day.

I looked over at Lubens. "Maybe we should think about sharing the gospel with these guys," I said in a depressed monotone. I didn't know what else to do—we had to pass the time somehow.

"Do you think they'll listen?" Lubens asked in a voice as dull as my own.

"I don't know, but we don't have anything else to do," I said.

We decided to offer to pray for the prisoners, and it was then that I then got some inspiration from God. I told the men that we wanted to pray for each of them, but we wanted to pray specifically. I asked whether they wanted us to pray for justice or mercy.

"If you are guilty, we can pray for mercy; if you are innocent, we can pray for justice." They liked the idea and so agreed.

One of the first men we talked to was a 58-year-old man accused of killing one of his sons. The night before, all the other prisoners had told us he was innocent—what man would kill his own son, they cried. We asked the man whether he would like mercy or justice. In front of everyone he said mercy. It was incredible that anybody would say mercy. It was most unusual for anyone in Haiti to admit his guilt, even if he was guilty.

Half of the men in the group said mercy, and half asked for justice. Some said both, because they were guilty to a degree but not to the extent that they had been charged.

One man started asking me a few questions. This gave me an opportunity to offer my testimony. As I was telling him how I had came to accept Christ, the prisoner next to me, a man called Tony, asked if he could accept Christ. He had already been in prison for thirteen months and hadn't even seen a judge. He had been arrested because he was part of a "manifestation" (a Creole name for a riot or protest) and was pulled out of the crowd to be made an example of.

When I asked whether anyone else wanted to accept Christ, six of the fourteen said yes. One man said he had to get rid of some voodoo things in his house before he could say yes. I told him we could deal with that all now by praying. He could throw the voodoo trinkets away when he got out of prison. I prayed a simple prayer with him, binding all the voodoo influence he had let into his life and his home. I then asked again if he wanted to accept Christ.

"Yes," he replied.

That made it seven people. The men all knelt on the prison floor, bowed their heads, and asked Jesus into their lives. It was definitely a first for me to lead people to the Lord sitting in my underwear in a stinking prison cell. I began to wonder whether this was the reason God had allowed me to go to prison.

# TWELVE

# Miracle

L E T me in! I demand to see my husband." It was Ingvild's voice I suddenly heard above the noises of the prison. "What other paper do you need? I have the paper you need," she shouted.

As soon as I realized she was there, I started yelling as loudly as I could. I didn't think the guards would let her in, and I wanted her to know I was okay.

"Ingvild! Ingvild!" I shouted, but the sound just echoed in the room.

All the men laughed at the desperation in my voice. Ingvild never even heard me.

Lubens was sitting on the floor next to me as I stood screaming for my wife. "Wow! Sound comes in, but nothing goes out of this place," he said with a big smile on his face.

I heard the gates suddenly open, and I saw Ingvild being taken into the center courtyard. As soon as I saw her, I felt like I was going to break. I was exhausted from having been up all night. All the prisoners started yelling and wolf-whistling at this beautiful white woman in front of them.

The guards made Ingvild stand in the middle of the courtyard under the bright sun. They then came over to my cell, opened it, and led me out.

"God, just don't let me cry," I prayed quickly under my breath.

We hugged, and I buried my head in her shoulder. She wanted to see my face to check to see if I had been beaten up. The guard said we could have only five minutes. Quickly I went over the list of people she needed to get ahold of. She had already contacted YWAMers all over the world who were praying about the situation. An officer of the U.S. consulate had just arrived and was at the base talking to the commissaire du gouvernement. Our five minutes went quickly, but as the guard came to take Ingvild away, the Norwegian Viking spirit came out in her, and she gave him a frightening stare as if to say, "You dare stop us." The guard stepped back and gave us a little longer. In Haitian culture it is the ultimate embarrassment for a man to be shouted at by a woman, and Haitian men try to avoid it at all costs.

Ingvild was just leaving as the guards were calling Lubens and me to be transported back to the courtroom. As we were leaving, the guards decided to handcuff us.

"You don't have to handcuff us. Have I ever tried to run from you? Where am I going to run?" I said.

"It's procedure. We have to do it," the guard replied.

The guards handcuffed my wrist to Lubens and then put us in the back of a pickup truck. They made Lubens sit on one side and me on the other, forcing us to sit with our hands held out. They then proceeded to drive us through the center of the city so that everyone could see us.

We got to the courthouse, where we were put into a holding cell until Commissaire Frenot called us. The cell looked like something for animals. It had no bathroom, and it was obvious that it had been used as a toilet. The smell was terrible. We stood waiting because the floor was too disgusting for us to sit down on. All of a sudden Lubens saw the national TV arrive, hoping to get footage of the white man who had beaten up the black man. He quickly shoved me back so that they couldn't get my picture. Lubens was incredibly wise in knowing how to protect me. He knew what not to allow to happen.

The guard wouldn't let YWAMers visit us at the cell to encourage us, but he let other people come in who would taunt us, saying, "You're dead. You're going to get necklaced (put inside a tire and set on fire). Even if you get out of here, you'll be driving down the road and there'll be a BAM, and you'll be shot."

I tried to ignore them, but they were beginning to get to me.

At last the U.S. consulate officer turned up. The officer was someone I knew, Alison Insley.

"Are you all right?" Alison asked.

"Yes," I replied.

Suddenly the guard said that Alison couldn't talk to me. Commissaire Frenot called me to his office. He wanted to listen to the accusations one more time to see whether they warranted a trial. Three more witnesses were brought in and heard. The commissaire then listened to Lubens and me tell our stories. The whole thing was a farce. Two out of the three witnesses against me had started with, "My friend told me." They hadn't even been there.

Alison was amazed at the lack of evidence. "It is not uncommon for Americans to be thrown into prison to try to kick them out of the country," she told me.

*Was this what the people were planning?* I wondered.

The unique thing about this case was that they didn't have a shred of evidence. The accusers' stories didn't make any sense, and all three witnesses had different versions of the story. However, our lawyer had been so intimidated by the people that he had kept quiet. Things started deteriorating.

"Okay, this warrants a trial. Let's schedule one five days from now," Commissaire Frenot finally said.

According to the Haitian calendar, that day would be a holiday.

"It's a trick," Lubens whispered to me. He knew that they were trying to keep us in prison for an indefinite period of time. My heart sank. I couldn't see any way out.

When Alison heard the date for the trial, she confronted the commissaire, but he wasn't listening. Finally she caught the commissaire's attention. The commissaire asked everyone to leave except for us. Frenot said he had to do what he had to do. Alison looked at me in shock. Nothing she had said could persuade Frenot to change his mind. "They are determined to keep you in prison," she said helplessly.

Frenot suggested I work with my lawyer to come up with money for bail. According to Haitian law it should be only about 5,000 gourdes, which is about $100. This time, however, they asked for $40,000.

I asked the commissaire for a private room so that I could discuss things with my lawyer, Alison, and my wife. Surprisingly he said yes and gave us a room where we all met together.

"They've set me up. I've been painted as a white man who beat up a black man. My ministry is ruined. I am going to be had one way or the other," I said to Alison.

Alison said she could not advise us what to do, but from her experience, people had to leave Haiti forever for less offenses than what I had been accused of. "At this time we don't see that there is any way you can stay in Haiti, regardless of how the situation comes out, even if you are proven innocent," she said sadly.

"Okay," I replied blankly. My world was crashing around me. I felt defeated.

"This can't be right. Is this the way God wants us to leave?" Ingvild asked.

I didn't know, but I did know that I didn't want to spend time behind bars in Haiti for something I didn't do. If God was going to do something, He needed to do it right away. We bowed our heads.

"God, we recognize that You are able to do miracles, but if You don't intervene here, we will take it as Your way of taking our family out of Haiti," I prayed.

We invited the beer seller's lawyer back in and asked him to talk about a plea bargain. He said we would have to give $40,000 and admit my guilt. We argued the amount down to $20,000.

"I can't listen to this anymore," Ingvild said, walking out in deep frustration.

All of a sudden she returned and said, "Terry, come with me."

"I can't, hon. I'm kind of occupied right now!" I said.

"A U.S. consulate officer has told me to come over and get you because you have been released," she said quickly.

She was speaking to me in English, and the lawyer had no idea what we were saying. Lubens and I stood up and walked out. The lawyer sat there looking confused. As I walked out, I saw a large crowd of people in the courthouse all glaring at us. There was no place to walk, it was so jammed.

"I don't know how we are going to get through this crowd. I barely got over here myself to get you," Ingvild said nervously.

It wasn't far—about fifty feet—back to the commissaire's office. I looked over to my left and my right and noticed that two policemen had been assigned to guard the door while we were inside. I looked at one of them and said, "You have to get me to the commissaire du gouvernement safely now!"

The crowd was made up mostly of gang members who were trying to intimidate me. The policeman looked over at his partner and all of a sudden the two officers jumped into action. They ran in front of us and moved everyone out of the way. One walked in front of us with an M16, and another walked behind us, protecting us all the way through the crowd to the commissaire du gouvernement's office. As we walked through the door, somebody slapped a paper on my chest. I looked down, wondering what it was. The consulate officer said, "That's your freedom paper. You're getting out of here!"

"What happened?" I asked incredulously.

Alison looked at me and said, "I have no idea what is going on. All I know is we are getting out of here!"

We sat in front of the commissaire du gouvernement's desk, Alison on one side of me and Lubens on the other, with Ingvild standing behind us. About eight police officers with M16s and shotguns were in the room with us.

The commissaire made some phone calls. "Okay, we are going to leave through the back door," he said after putting the phone down. He told us we would all go in different cars.

"No, we want Terry in the car with us," Alison said.

He agreed.

I was put in the consulate's car. Lubens was put in a police car between two policemen with shotguns to protect him. Commissaire Frenot ordered two police officers to escort Ingvild home and stay with her until I returned or, if I didn't return home, to escort my family out of the city. As the cars drove out the front gate, a huge crowd of angry people were all shouting and watching.

Alison was sitting in the front seat of the consulate's car. "Oh no! Bury him! Bury him!" Alison said when she saw the crowd. The two marines who sat on either side of me pushed me to the floor and put their arms over me so that no one could see that I was in the car with them.

We drove back to the prison, and I was legally released. I had been fingerprinted when I went into the prison, and now I had to be fingerprinted to show that I was released or I would become an escaped convict. The commissaire hoped that taking me back to the prison would trick the people into thinking I was being locked up again.

"Now are you happy?" Commissaire Frenot asked as I was about to leave.

"Yes, I am very happy!" I replied with a big smile on my face.

"Okay, then. I am done. I'm gone," he said, leaving the room.

Alison drove us back to our house. When we arrived, she suddenly told us we had two minutes to get everything we needed and to get out.

"Two minutes! This is everything I own. There is no way I can pack everything in two minutes," I replied.

"Terry, we cannot guarantee your safety. You need to get out of here with your family while you can. We will give you escort, but you have to come now," Alison said sternly.

"Then you are going to have to leave, because I can't do that. We will just have to trust God," I said with a shrug of my shoulders.

"You understand that we cannot guarantee your safety if you do this," she replied.

"Yes, I understand," I said. "We will leave tomorrow morning first thing. I will call you as soon as we get to Port-au-Prince."

God had just released me from prison. Ingvild had peace that He would look after us overnight. Alison then left, as the U.S. consulate had told her to get out of the city.

We held a staff meeting and told all the YWAM staff what was going on. Staff members Jonathan and Laurie Irons were left in charge because Brian was out of the country. The base did not seem to be under any threat. The gangs were just after me and Lubens.

Early the next morning I left with my family and Lubens. We didn't know whether we would ever be able to come back. The U.S. consulate had made it very clear that we were going to have to leave the country. We stayed in a hotel in Port-au-Prince. Only a few people knew where we were. Bill Landis and Kent Norell flew over immediately. They thought they were coming over to bail me out of jail and were pleasantly surprised to meet me at the airport. They paid for our hotel and prayed with us. We contacted the U.S. consulate, who wanted a full report. The first thing the consulate wanted to know was when we were leaving and whether we had a flight booked.

"I have invested too much in this country to leave this quickly. Let's see what happens," I said to them.

We had watched the news and were amazed that there had been no media coverage on the story. This was a good sign.

We went back to the hotel. The U.S. consulate was doing everything it could to get us to leave, putting pressure on Lubens to convince us to go. We knew we couldn't run in this way. We had to look to God.

On the third day Jonathan phoned us with shocking news. Commissaire Frenot had sent a letter to the base for me and Lubens in which he apologized for what had happened. He asked us to return to the city and promised us security if we did return.

We were amazed. Lubens, streetwise as he is, was concerned that it was a trick. The consulate agreed with Lubens. I prayed about it and felt we had to give it a go. This was our only chance to go back. So after only three days in Port-au-Prince, we headed back to St. Marc.

We prayed about going in separate cars, with Ingvild and the kids coming behind. God spoke to Ingvild from Zechariah 8:13, and she knew we would be safe. We drove together into the city. We went right through the zone where all the gangs were. Everybody stopped to watch us drive through. We didn't know whether their looks were hostile or if they were simply amazed that we were back.

While we had been gone, people from our zone and near our mission had begun to stand up for me. "Terry would never have done the things he has been accused of. We all know this is a trick," they had said.

The St. Marc officials were accused of trying to get money out of me. Things were starting to turn in our favor. This amazed the consulate. Even during the hearing, the officers had been amazed at how people were speaking up for us. Alison had said that she had never seen Haitians defend an American the way we had been defended.

We drove into the mission to see the staff and let them know we were back. As I was closing the gate, a man drove up. He sat in his car checking me out. I felt intimidated, as he was a big guy and I was on edge because of what had happened. He was wearing lots of gold chains and reminded me of Mr. T from the A-Team.

The man called me over to him. I wasn't sure this was such a good idea, but for some reason I decided to walk over. I was walking slowly, trying to look into his lap to see if he had a gun.

"Yeah?" I said as I got near.

"I want you to know I know what happened to you. You don't have anything to worry about," he said, then put his car into gear and drove off.

The strange thing was that nobody knew who he was, and nobody has seen him since. Later I wondered if perhaps he was a guardian angel.

The next day Bill, Kent, and I drove around the city to scout out the land and see the people's reactions to me. Everything was quiet. People were just staring at us. It was quite spooky and almost felt like a ghost town.

"Let's go to the prison!" I suddenly said to Bill and Kent.

"What do you want to do there?" a shocked Bill replied.

I wanted to show them the horrendous condition I had lived in. While we were in prison, Lubens and I had discussed the improvements that needed to be made. I didn't know if the guards would let us in, but I had to try. We knocked on the prison gate, but it was closed. As we turned to leave, the porthole suddenly opened and a guard looked out. When he saw me, his eyes grew very big.

"May I come in?" I asked.

Not knowing what to do, the guard opened the gate up and let us in. I began to show Bill and Kent the cell and where we had to bathe. Suddenly a very concerned inspector (who was the head of the prison) came running out. Before I could say anything he shouted, "We didn't treat you bad. We treated you well. We didn't do anything to hurt you."

I just smiled and nodded. "Yes, I know that, but the conditions of this prison are terrible."

In defense he simply said, "They don't give us any money."

"That is why I am here to figure out how we can fix this prison up. The question is, Will you let me help you?" I asked.

The inspector smiled. "You were in this prison. We can trust you."

The guards and the inspector saw that I was coming back to help them and not to get revenge. They thankfully agreed to let us do whatever we wanted. Our campaign to rebuild the prison had started.

# THIRTEEN

# Unity and Action

CALL a pastors' meeting," I felt God say one morning as I was praying about rebuilding the prison. Before this time we had had only one or two pastors' meetings, and only about fourteen pastors had come. I starting to contact the pastors I knew, and we arranged a meeting that week.

I wanted to speak to the pastors about what had happened to me in prison and dispel the rumors that were going around. People didn't know what was true and what wasn't. Many believed I was a member of the CIA, because they couldn't understand why I had been released from prison so rapidly. Also, when we were in prison, Lubens had been told to tell me to admit to being part of the CIA and I would be released right away. This was a trap, as the officials knew it wasn't true, and it would have given them proof that I was lying.

Forty-five pastors came to the first meeting. I had never before seen such a large group of church leaders gathered in one place in St. Marc. I told the story of the prison and gave details about what had happened, verifying that I was not FBI or CIA. Pastor Wilson, who had known us since we first came to St. Marc, stood up saying, "If they are going to do this to an American missionary, what hope do we have as Haitian pastors?"

A soberness came over the meeting as the pastors realized that our only strength was in unity. Their first reaction was to do a "manifestation"—a normal Haitian response. They would go down to the courthouse with signs and would picket, or they would call the mayor to attend a special meeting with representation of all the pastors and demand an apology. But God had already shown me what to do before the meeting had even started. He had spoken to me through the book of Nehemiah about rebuilding the walls, serving the city.

"This is not how we need to handle this. The reason they threw us in prison is that our message is so strong," I said.

Instead of stopping what we were doing and starting something else, we needed to continue with greater force. The gang activity on the land we had gotten from Freole had ended. Gangs were rapidly losing their influence. Some of the voices that had ruled in fear no longer had such significance. It had been heard in the neighborhood that people had begun to say to the gangs, "We don't want to listen to you. The mission is here now."

The gangs had seen the soccer tournament as an opportunity to knock out me and Lubens, whom they saw as my right-hand man. They wanted to see the YWAM base abandoned so that they could obtain the land again and regain their authority in the zone. That was the root of the issue.

I said to the pastors, "We don't need to do a manifestation. We need to continue to preach the strong message we have been preaching. We need to be like Godzilla invading Tokyo—an overwhelming power that overshadows the zone so the enemy is on the run. We remain on the offense and they on the defense. We need to bless, not attack."

I pointed out the book of Nehemiah. "As spiritual fathers of this city, we need to be thinking about what we can do to see the city regain vision. The reality is, apart from God there is no vision. The vision will have to come through us," I said.

The meeting had an air of excitement to it. We felt like we were beginning the process of becoming a unified church.

News of the meeting spread, and a month later we had a second pastors' meeting. By that time we had drawn a makeshift street map of St. Marc. We located a number of churches that wanted to be a part of this new network. By our second meeting, ninety-four pastors were in attendance. I understood from some senior pastors that they had kept their associate pastors back at their churches because pastors were coming out of the mountains to participate in the meeting. One man said he had twelve pastors waiting back at his church. When they came, he told them that the network wasn't expecting so many, so he would go to the meeting and come back and report on the outcome.

We began to formulate a plan for communication if one of us was in danger or arrested, coming up with a way we could communicate effectively and quickly. The city was broken up into four sections, north, south, east, and west, and we assigned a leader over each section who would be responsible for his part of the city. We also decided we needed to show a strong presence, so we held a crusade focusing on solidarity. It was held on our land, and three thousand people came.

We kept our focus and eyes on the prison and what we could do there. I was able to get authorization for the pastors to visit the prisoners. The first time we went in with the pastors' group on a Sunday morning to have church, we asked if the guards would let everybody out into the courtyard. They agreed, even though it was something they wouldn't normally do. At the first church service, thirty-four out of the one hundred prisoners accepted Christ.

Both the prisoners and the guards were complaining that the prison had no clean water, so we drilled a well. The only water the prison had was in a cistern. Because the well would take time to drill, first we put in a pump with a pressurized water system for the cistern. This provided showers. We built a showering area in the back and cleaned up all the rubbish, getting rid of the rats in the process. We soon realized that we were so focused on trying to make the prison more sanitary for the prisoners that we weren't aware that the guards themselves were living under similar conditions. The only difference between them and the prisoners was that they weren't locked in at night. The guards had begun to get a little frustrated. We built them a toilet and shower facility with a porcelain toilet. This elevated the guards' living standards enough in the guards' minds and allowed us to have the freedom to continue to improve the conditions for the prisoners. We painted the prison inside and out and added a second electricity line, allowing the prison to have virtually twenty-four-hour electricity for the first time.

We also were given permission to set up a chaplain's office at the prison. Volunteers were allowed to visit the prison and pass messages to family members of the prisoners. This was important, since some of the prisoners had been arrested in St. Marc but their families weren't from the city and didn't know where their relatives were.

Prisoners were not permitted to go before a judge unless they were wearing shoes. Some prisoners had been arrested wearing only shorts and sandals. Sandals didn't count. As a result, these prisoners were not allowed to see the judge. The pastors let us know when these items were lacking, and we kept a supply of shoes and clothing to help the process along.

Normally the prisoners got two meals a day, one at about 10:00 AM and one at 4:00 PM. Sometimes they got only one meal, sometimes none, depending on how the government had set up its budgeting. Church groups began to go into the prison and cook meals at scheduled times.

We learned that two weeks after I had been in prison, five of the seven prisoners who had accepted Christ had been released. The other two were released in a month. Even Tony, the man who had been there for thirteen months, was released after two months.

About the same time, Mercy Ships had contacted me and decided that they would like to visit St. Marc if the door was open. I took the proposal to the pastors, and we formed a committee to ask the mayor if the ship could come into the wharf to see whether it would fit and could stay for a week or so. I explained that the ship would provide medical and developmental assistance to the people of St. Marc. The mayor was very enthusiastic and said he would do all he could to help. This meeting was the beginning of my relationship with Mayor Paul Pollyx.

A few days later I returned to the mayor's office to check on the progress of the ship. I met Paul as he was leaving. He asked me to walk with him in the city park, which was right across from his office. The park was about an acre and was filled with trash. Everything in it—from the lights to the benches—was broken. The grass was dead, and weeds were growing everywhere.

As we started to walk toward the park, suddenly the beer seller who had accused me of beating him up saw me and began to yell and mock me. I tried to ignore him, hoping he would go away. I was embarrassed that the beer seller was yelling at me in front of the mayor. The seller had been mocking me off and on ever since I had been in prison six months earlier. At the same time he was ridiculed by the people. He had been named "The Man of Twenty Thousand" because he claimed he "got $20,000 out of Terry Snow."

Paul looked over at me and realized I was annoyed with the man. The mayor's bodyguard was walking with us, carrying an automatic Luger (like a pistol machine gun). As we walked through the park, Paul glanced at his bodyguard and pointed to the beer seller. Suddenly the bodyguard left us and went straight up to the yelling beer seller. The guard spoke to him quietly, and suddenly the beer seller turned and ran. He never mocked me again.

As we continued to walk in the park, Paul looked around and said, "Isn't this park sad? It should be beautiful."

I agreed. "Yeah. Why isn't the fountain working?" I asked. An old fountain sat in the park, and I had never seen it run from the time I moved to St. Marc in 1991. Later I found out it hadn't worked since 1985. "Why don't you do something about it?"

Paul shrugged his shoulders. "No one knows how to fix it. I was talking to someone about it today. We thought about getting rid of it."

Since I knew that this would be a missed opportunity, I said, "Why don't you let me fix it!"

Paul looked dubious. "Can you fix it?"

Confidently I replied, "Sure I can!" I had never fixed a fountain in my life. I knew nothing about fountains.

Paul realized he had nothing to lose and agreed to let me fix it. I went with Roberteau Desilorme and Fiance Alexis, YWAM staff members, and we started digging around the fountain to get to the plumbing. The fountain was filled with burned rubble and trash. People had been regularly using it as a bathroom as well. It was a mess. We finally got it all cleaned out, and I went home. When Ingvild met me at the door and got one whiff of me, she said, "Undress *outside!*" She wouldn't let me even walk into the house, because my clothes were so filthy and stank.

I still did not know how to fix the fountain. All the plumbing was destroyed. I could see how the pipes went through it, but other than that, the fountain was just a hollow drum shell. I began to ask God how to fix it. Immediately He began to give me inspiration. He reminded me of the man who had helped us build the swimming pool.

*What is a fountain anyway,* I thought. *It's nothing more than a swimming pool, the filtration, channeling, and replenishing of water from one source to another.*

We redeveloped the fountain under the same engineering ideas and concepts that God had taught me through the building of the swimming pool. It turned out that the pool was more than a simple blessing. It was training for the restoration of the fountain.

When we turned on the water, the people were mesmerized by the fountain. It had been almost two decades since the people of St. Marc had seen it work. When it came on, they just gazed at it and took pictures of it. It became a new photo opportunity. The street children were bathing in it, and drinking out of it. The water was purer than anything they had. The car washers in the area were using it for car washing. The project had been worth all the sweat and tears.

By that time in YWAM we had been able to feed and clothe people, show them dramas, and give them crusades. You name it, we had done it. But I can't ever remember people coming up to me and saying, "Thank you, thank you, thank you" from the depths of their hearts as they did with the fountain. It gave so much pride to the city of St. Marc. I felt that the fountain had become a prophetic statement of life springing forth into the heart of the city.

Because of the success of the fountain, it was easier for us to get permission to help in other ways. Paul saw us fix the fountain, then cut the grass and clear away all the rubbish in the park. Winning the trust of the mayor had come out of serving. After we had fixed the fountain, Paul showed me other areas around the city that needed improvement. I could see that he saw me as a funding opportunity. I was a white American and therefore, in his eyes, rich. Driving the mayor back to his office, I parked the car outside and said, "Paul, you have to understand something about me. Anything and everything I do is by the hand and the will of God. I am not a wealthy man, but I have a wealthy God. You need to understand that all the glory will go to God if I am a part of it."

Since I knew he wasn't a Christian, I didn't know how he would take this. Paul was very quiet. He didn't say a word and just got out of the car. That same week I visited him again to ask him a question. I arrived at his office and waited with the receptionist, as he was in a meeting. Suddenly the door to his office opened, and Paul saw that I was waiting. Immediately he stopped the meeting and said to the man guarding the door, "See that man right there? Don't ever make him wait for me."

Paul immediately called me in and asked what he could do for us.

Embarrassed, I said it could wait. It was not so important that he had to stop the meeting for us. But Paul was adamant and asked again what he could do for us.

As time went on my relationship with Paul Pollyx grew, and I continued to share the gospel with him.

# FOURTEEN

# The Power of God Is Here

IT WAS a hot summer's day. The pastors had been called to a special meeting to discuss what they could do as a response to the annual Boukman Pact celebrations that were taking place later that month. Sweating from the summer heat outside, we sat in a small classroom inside a church in the center of St. Marc.

A reporter from a national Haitian newspaper had come to the meeting, curious to see whether the pastors were concerned about the kidnapping of a child in Port-au-Prince. A young baby had been taken from the hospital by a witch doctor from St. Marc. We all knew that the baby had been taken as a human sacrifice.

The reporter asked for our reaction to the event. The pastors shrugged their shoulders. They acknowledged the sadness of the situation, but many had resigned themselves to the fact that this is what happens in Haiti. The story had touched me deeply. I was incensed at the apathy among the group.

"Has God brought me to Haiti to weep for your children because you have forgotten how?" I asked with passion.

The pastors were challenged by my words more than I had antici-
pated. We started to plan an event to make a stand. God spoke to me
through the Bible story of Gideon, of how Gideon and his men had surrounded the Midianite camp, lit torches, and praised and shouted to the
Lord. The enemy had been filled with fear and fled (Judges 7:15–21). I
felt that we should do the same, and the pastors agreed. On August 14
at 5:00 AM we met to pray for the city. Over a thousand people then
marched around the outskirts, praying for St. Marc. We preached and
prayed in the center of the park until noon. At four o'clock in the afternoon we all met in the park again. The atmosphere was electric with
excitement and anticipation. Pastor Chavanne Jeune had arrived to
preach. He had a camera crew with him, and his preaching was broadcast over the whole of Haiti. Our small act was reaching the nation.
Illioney told the story of Gideon and then separated everyone into six
teams, depending on which zone each team wanted to pray over. I stayed
in the park as everyone marched off carrying torches and shouting their
praises to the Lord. When each team got to its prayer point, it would
let off a huge firework to let us all know it had arrived and had started
praying. The night sky was awash with beautiful colors, as one by one
the teams lit their fireworks and began to pray for their city.

I then set off a display of fireworks from the city park. This communicated to the people on the mountains that everybody was ready.
The intercessors let out a shout, declaring Jesus is Lord over the city.

I received a few excited phone calls from prayers up in the mountains. One YWAM staff member Rosvelt (RoRo) Thomacin called, his
voice high with excitement. "Terry," he said. "Terry, God is moving. The
power of God is here."

Everybody sensed it. God was doing something.

At about 10:30 PM a few others and I packed up the sound system
and made our way home. Later we found out we had just missed a joyful crowd of people returning to the park. We had assumed that everyone would go home since it was late. Instead, filled with joy, people had
marched all the way back from the mountains to the park.

It was with much excitement that we heard some amazing news the
next day. The famous Bois Caiman tree was dead. The tree was in the far
north of Haiti. Underneath the tree, it was said, Boukman had made his

pact with the devil on August 14, 1791. Every year since then, voodoo witch doctors would go to the tree around the same date to make sacrifices. At some point the tree had been hit by lightning and split in two. Out of the dead tree, another one, with cruel-looking thorns on it, had grown. The witch doctors would perform their ceremony at the tree and then climb up it. Shoeless and shirtless, they would come down without a scratch and claim that this showed the power of their voodoo god.

In 2001 a Haitian pastor named Joel Jeune convinced a landowner to let him purchase the land next to the tree. This gave Christians legal access to pray against the tree and the evil associated with it. The voodoo priests became incensed by the pastor who had bought the land, saying that he was ruining their magic. The police had to put the pastor in prison for a night during the times of the sacrifices for his own safety, or he would have been killed.

It was August 2003 when we heard that the tree had died and there had been no annual sacrifice. We discussed the story as a staff, and Brian and Illioney offered to make the journey north to see for themselves what had happened. They drove four and a half hours from St. Marc to get to the site. They asked a receptionist at a hotel two miles from the tree what had happened. "We had reservations for several government officials who were supposed to take part in the ceremony, but they never turned up," she said.

Another employee at the hotel said that because the churches had gotten together and prayed, Satan had been chased away from the land.

Brian and Illioney decided to make the short journey to see the tree for themselves. As they drove down the narrow dirt road, they saw two banners spread across the road saying, "Voodoo, the source of our liberty."

When they arrived at the tree, they saw that it was large and impressive, but dead. The very place that marks the source and root of Haitian liberty was dead. The area around the tree was fertile and well watered, with hundreds of healthy trees, only this one tree was dead.

Illioney went to talk to the pastor at the church nearby.

"Big sacrifices were planned, but not even an ant died!" the pastor said with a big smile. He said that in the past two years sacrifices had been made at the tree by two witch doctors so that fire would break out in the church and kill the pastor and any believers worshiping there. However, the sacrifices hadn't worked, and not long after, both witch doctors had died.

We were amazed at what God had done. Over the past few years there has been a decrease in voodoo and voodoo sacrifices in Haiti. The tide is slowly turning.

It was early evening on August 28, 2003, when the rain began to fall. We were just finishing the final pastors' meeting before the crusade. There didn't seem to be anything unusual about the rain, since we were right in the middle of the rainy season. But the rain continued through the night. By the next morning we heard a loud commotion outside in the streets. We found out there had been a great flood in the city.

"It can't be that bad, because we haven't been touched," I said to Ingvild when we heard the news. But as I drove closer to the center of town, I was shocked at the devastation. Mud was everywhere. Water had been flowing through the city park three feet above the ground. A body was found floating through the park. We were told that many people had drowned, but no one knew how many.

The rain had poured down on one spot high in the mountains. The water had drained into the river that ran through St. Marc. It had come down in waves, causing a flash flood.

The water was now just below the crest of a bridge that was normally twenty feet above the water. People were dismayed and shocked as they watched the water and debris flowing through their city. I found out later they were watching for bodies of friends and relatives.

Pierre-Richard and I drove on out of the city to an area called La Scierie, which was supposed to have been the worst affected by the flood. When we got there, we met the mayor and two of his assistants. Their faces had drained of color.

"How bad is it?" I asked.

"Really bad," the mayor replied, shaking his head.

The kay pòv (poor houses), built of banana leaves and mud, had all been washed away. I saw what had once been a cement house. All that was left was its foundation. The locals said that a family of five had lived in the house. They had tried to get their possessions out before the water came. The villagers screamed at them not to go back, but the father insisted they had to get their things. He made all his family go inside to help him. Suddenly, when they were all inside, the whole house crumbled and was washed away. The family was never found again.

I turned and saw a young girl, covered from head to toe in mud, leaning against a tree. It looked like she had been wallowing in the mud. She had a look of devastation on her face. She gazed into the sky, no words to describe her grief, exhaustion, and hunger.

I realized that to the left of me the children had dug up a city water pipe and were trying to suck the fresh water out of it. The people were in desperate need of basic life essentials: fresh water, clothes, and food. I talked with the mayor and locals about what we could do, but no one had any answers. We had no idea how many people had been affected by the flood.

At that time YWAM Haiti had never done any kind of organized relief effort as a mission. We had brought in medical teams, but only on a small scale.

The day after the flood I learned that the city had no more money for the bulldozer to clear the mud. We had heard no word from Port-au-Prince about what money they might send. We had to do something.

I called an emergency pastors' meeting. We started responding to the needs of the people. We did a count of every house that was destroyed or damaged. Just under seven hundred homes had been affected by the flood. YWAM came up with an ID card system. This gave us an idea of where each flood victim had lived and how many people were in each family. It also stated whether the house was rented or owned and how damaged it was.

Some of the pastors thought we should cancel our upcoming crusade. But we prayed and decided to make the crusade a rally point. We asked the people of St. Marc to bring clothes, pots and pans, and furniture to assist the flood victims. From the offering we were able to raise $1,700. This was outstanding. It was the largest offering ever taken among the united churches of St. Marc. In addition we were able to clothe over two thousand people from what was donated. We also ended up rebuilding twenty-two homes, assisting in the repairs of fifty houses, and cleaning the mud out of many more.

Christian Aid Ministries contacted us saying they had six hundred relief boxes we could use, so we coordinated with them to get the boxes out to the people. Because we had done an effective job with the ID cards, we were able to hand out the food boxes to the families that needed them most. The boxes contained oil, rice, beans, vitamins, toothbrushes, toothpaste, soap, milk, and much more. With each box we handed out two buckets and a bar of soap so that people could wash their clothes. From all the appeals we were sending out we received four trailer loads of clothing. We were able to give clothing to every person who had been in the flood.

I met with Mayor Paul to discuss what was happening. "The government gave $35,000 to assist the flood victims, but it is obvious that the church is able to do more. I don't understand this," he said.

The church and YWAM had distributed over $150,000 in aid to the flood victims. Through our acts of service in the midst of the flood and restoration of the fountain we gained incredible influence and favor with the people of St. Marc.

As I walked through the homes in the devastated neighborhoods, people now knew me by name. They no longer saw me as a foreigner but as a friend, a friend who helped when they needed help. They were now open to hearing the gospel because they had seen it in action.

# FIFTEEN

# A City Transformed

ORIGINALLY the idea had been that the pastors' network would eventually dissolve, but because YWAM had become neutral ground, we didn't want to stop the good work that was taking place. We realized that the network was not just for internal ministry and encouragement among the pastors; there was already a group called the League of Pastors for that purpose. The network was for equipping and mobilizing the pastors to reach the masses.

It wasn't always so easy, however. In the early days of the network there was a lot of friction. Ridiculous doctrinal disagreements would arise. To avoid any confusion, we decided to run the network on the YWAM statement of faith:

*We are an international movement of Christians from many denominations dedicated to presenting Jesus personally to this generation, to mobilizing as many as possible to help in this task, and to the training and equipping of believers for their part in fulfilling the Great Commission. As citizens of God's kingdom, we are called to love, worship, and obey our Lord, to love and serve His Body, the Church, and to present the whole gospel for the whole person throughout the whole world.*

*We believe that the Bible is God's inspired and authoritative word, revealing that Jesus Christ is God's son; that people are created in God's image; that He created us to have eternal life through Jesus Christ; that although all people have sinned and come short of God's glory, God has made salvation possible through the death on the cross and resurrection of Jesus Christ; that repentance, faith, love and obedience are fitting responses to God's initiative of grace toward us; that God desires all people to be saved and to come to the knowledge of the truth; and that the Holy Spirit's power is demonstrated in and through us for the accomplishment of Christ's last commandment, "...Go ye into all the world and preach the gospel to every creature" (Mark 16:15) (King James Version).*

All the pastors, whatever their denomination, agreed on it. The statement was the glue that kept us all together and ended bickering.

To keep the pastors in harmony, we focused on community projects together. We looked for projects that were on neutral ground and were not associated with any one church. Together we worked on restoring the prison and dug wells for different zones. We held seminars on the YWAM base, and the pastors began to work more closely together. For the first time pastors from smaller churches felt that they were equal with the pastors from the larger churches. They were able to air their frustrations and have their voices heard.

A unity was brought about as a result of the acknowledgment that we were all serving the same Lord. Consequently, St. Marc now has a unified church. There are at least thirty different denominations, but they are just different tastes, different colors. Before the pastors' network, new Christians would come to me and ask which church to go to. "One church says this, the other says that. So who is saying the truth?" they would ask. People didn't know who was speaking the truth, and they saw a great division in the church.

At one of our meetings I asked the pastors what we should do next. Pastor Renaud Guillaume said he felt that we needed to build gates at the three entrance points to the city as a security checkpoint. I started getting excited about his suggestion, reflecting back on the book of Nehemiah through which God had spoken. Security was one of the main problems in St. Marc. Theft was common. It was time for the church to play a more significant role in the concerns of the city so that the people would realize the church was present and cared about them. By putting these gates in, we could help the police monitor who was coming in and out of the city. We hoped that having a welcoming entrance to the city would make St. Marc more inviting for visitors. It was going to be a huge task.

A committee was formed, and we presented the project to the mayor and asked for his permission to build the gates. The mayor was very welcoming and friendly. He said he had a similar idea and would help us all he could. Mayor Paul embraced the pastors' network and was very open with us.

With this encouragement, pastors began to do things they had never done before. They planned a soccer game to raise money for the gates. All the pastors, including me, played in the match. We sold tickets, and the event attracted a huge crowd. Our most senior pastor, a very old, grey-haired man named Xavier, ran after the ball like a young man. The crowd went wild. After the match we held a crusade and took up an offering for the building of the gates. In the end much of the money came from outside donors, but the churches gave generously.

The people of the city were also generous to us. A hardware supply business gave us materials at cost. The government donated the sand and rock we would need, and some church members gave their labor.

I sensed that if any character or integrity was to be won back to the church of Jesus Christ in the city, we would have to finish this seemingly impossible task. It wasn't easy. We had to get approval from the Haiti Public Works Department (TCPC) and the National Electricity Company (EDH). Completing the first gate was a great victory because everybody had said we couldn't do it.

One day when the first gate was nearly finished, I was driving through the city. *If a stranger came into the city of St. Marc, how would he or she know that the church was alive?* I wondered. This thought came out of the blue, but I was sure that it was God speaking to me. The church buildings I saw were filthy dirty and unpainted. Overshadowing them were bright and colorful voodoo flags flying. Images of voodoo were everywhere, but I didn't see the presence of the church. This really bothered me, and I began to pray about it.

At our next network meeting I challenged the pastors and asked them what we could do to show a greater presence of the church. As I spoke, the pastors began to see the problem. We came up with the idea of putting a monument in the park, one that would cause children in the next generation to ask, "Why is this thing here?" We decided on a large granite stone of some sort to symbolize "The Rock" that is immovable. I had seen a similar image in Norway when our family visited some of Ingvild's relatives. I had been impacted by it and thought it was very beautiful. It had a plaque on it saying, "This church is founded in God and will not be moved." The pastors also decided on a sixteen-foot-wide image of a Bible open to Exodus at the Ten Commandments.

A few months later I traveled to Pennsylvania. Through Paul Martin I had found a Christian company—Weaver Memorials Rock of Ages. The company located a stone, and we had it engraved with "*Christ for St. Marc, St. Marc for Christ 2004 New Beginnings.*"

This was a prophetic gesture of what we believed would be taking place at the beginning of the year 2004. We knew that 2004 would mark the end of the two hundred years dedicated to the devil plus the thirteen years until independence had been declared. We also felt that 2004 would be a significant time in the history of Haiti, and we wanted to be ready for all God was going to do. When I came to Mayor Paul to ask if we could put a Christian monument in the park, something that had never been done before in the history of Haiti, he said without doubt and without flinching, "No problem. The park is yours."

We hoped to finish the first gate and the monument at the same time. We had just completed building the basketball Sports Evangelistic Arena on rum-factory land. The arena could seat 1,780 people on bleachers. On September 15, 2003, we would dedicate the gate, the monument, and the sports arena with a grand crusade.

Driving out of the mission campus on the day before the dedication, I could see grey clouds forming. We were planning to have a small ceremony to place the rock on its pedestal in front of the Ten Commandments.

*Oh no, the rain is coming,* I thought. Strangely it looked like the rain was coming from the northwest. Usually rain came from the northeast. I hurriedly told everyone that we needed to get down to the park quickly because in Haiti it never rains just a little; it comes in buckets. Our ceremony would be ruined.

I was very concerned and raced down to the park. By the time we all got there, there was a thick cloud covering. The good thing was that this cooled everything down, but I knew it was about to pour at any minute. Time was of the essence. Everyone gathered and watched the huge tractor slowly coming down the road carrying the rock to the park. As the tractor extended the boom so that we could push the rock out and then set it gently on its pedestal, it began to drizzle. There was no downpour, just a soft, refreshing, dew-like rain.

Bill Landis, along with many others who had invested time and finances into the mission, had flown in to join us for the dedication. We all sensed the presence of God. We gently placed the rock on its pedestal so that the writing was in the right place and everything was angled correctly. All of a sudden the drizzle just stopped, and the cloud disappeared, as if it had dissolved. Everybody had a sense that God had shown up to see the mounting for the stone.

We worked all night to finish the gate and the monument. We had difficulties getting the sign "Welcome to St. Marc" on top of the gate. The sign was so large that we had to bring in a special tractor and crane to hook it up.

That night, after the gate was finished, we and some of our partners went down to the monument with a spotlight and hung the letters of the Ten Commandments. This was a challenge, as they were written in French. Illioney came with us to make sure we got the spellings right and didn't put the sentences on backwards.

As dawn arrived on Sunday, September 15, everything was finished. The sign was finished, the monument was done. I wasn't sure what was going to happen or who would turn up. The gate was a good distance from the city. At eight o'clock I got into the car at the base with a few other leaders, and we started driving out to the gate. I began to see people walking. I could tell they were Christians, since they were holding their Bibles. The closer we got to the gate, the more people we saw.

At the gate the whole area was crowded. The police arrived to direct the traffic, since many people were blocking the road.

We dedicated the city entrance, asking God to put up an angelic barrier along with the physical barrier that had been built. We asked that God would protect our city, and we recognized that God was the One who had given us the strength to build the gate. As we finished with the prayers, everyone turned back toward the center of St. Marc. The procession was led by musicians playing on a large truck with a giant sound system on the back. The residents of St. Marc cut branches from the trees and began to wave them and throw them into the streets. They were shouting and rejoicing. The only time I had ever seen anything like it was when the former dictator Duvalier had left the country and Haiti was liberated.

The roads were full of green branches. The inhabitants of St. Marc marched on. There were so many people that you couldn't see the end of the line. Tap-tap (mass-transit cab) drivers were going mad because they couldn't get their pickups or buses through and onto their next stops. But when they realized what was happening and saw all the tree limbs, they calmed down and waited for a way to get around the crowd. There was total joy in the city.

Eventually everyone arrived at the monument. We dedicated it to God and asked that He would help us as a city to live by the Ten Commandments.

That evening over seven thousand people turned up at our Evangelistic Arena. The arena was on an acre-and-a-quarter plot of land.

"There is no way everyone will fit in," Mel Weaver said in disbelief.

"This is Haiti!" I said with a smile.

"I'll believe it when I see it," he replied.

That night he came up to me and said, "I believe it!'

People were full of joy celebrating. We finished the day off with fireworks, and God had been given all the glory.

# SIXTEEN

# War

AT THE end of 2003, as we began to anticipate the change that would take place in Haiti in 2004, things were starting to heat up politically. One day in November 2003 a Haitian man named Ronald Doufen, whose nickname was Blac Ronald (also known as Blac), visited me at the mission with a friend of his. I had no idea who he was, but he said that he was seeking a way out of the country and wanted to see whether I could help him with the visa. Since he seemed nice enough and was kind to me, I said I would do what I could. Unknown to me, he was notorious for committing murders and assassinations while serving with Aristide's elite police force. Some people in the city recognized Blac Ronald and saw him entering the base. Blac didn't get his visa, and I heard rumors that he wasn't happy about that.

I left St. Marc for a few weeks in January 2004 to go to Jamaica for a Foundational Community Development School at the Jamaica YWAM base. On the plane home I felt I was going back into some dangerous situations. I had been given a prophetic word in Jamaica that my life was in danger, and the base had told me on the phone that while I had been away, rumors had been going around that someone was going to try to take my life. People in the city were plotting against me, but we didn't know who or why. It was with much caution that I landed in Port-au-Prince. We decided to arrange a decoy. It would look like I was being picked up, but then my ride would leave, and I would sneak out later.

By this time we had found out that Blac was a known assassin, notorious for the blood he had spilled in Citi Soleil. We didn't know whether *he* was plotting against me because he hadn't gotten his visa or people in the city thought I was working with him and therefore *they* wanted me dead. Different Haitians from St. Marc were telling our staff members that I needed to watch out. We were hearing strange noises on our telephones; it sounded like the phones were being tapped.

Haiti is known as a country in constant turmoil, the poorest country in the Western Hemisphere, and a country that practices voodoo. The civil unrest of 2004 had come about under the presidency of Jean-Bertrand Aristide. Gonaives, a city in the north, had begun to rebel against Aristide's leadership. A rebel gang called the Cannibals had taken control of the city. The Cannibals were originally part of Aristide's political party, but he had betrayed them, so they had turned against him. Their rising up sparked the war that ultimately divided the north of the country from the south, with St. Marc on the dividing line. This scenario had happened once before, in 1806, when the newly independent nation of Haiti was formed under the government of Henri Christophe and General Pétion. A civil war had broken out between the two leaders in the north and the south, and the dividing line was St. Marc. Henri Christophe eventually died, and the battle lines slowly dissolved, again uniting Haiti. It seemed like history was replaying itself nearly two hundred years later.

During this time of civil unrest, Blac came back to see me. He said he had been made the commissaire of St. Marc. He would control CIMO, an elite police force for the president. He had had training from the military. He was running the city with direct orders from Aristide, working with Député Mayette, putting order in the city from a "legal" standpoint.

Portail Montrouis (our zone) was anti-Aristide, and the people had blocked off all the roads to protect themselves against the Bale Wouze, the armed force behind Aristide's party in St. Marc. Our base was essentially between those who were for Aristide and those who were against him. Our whole zone was blocked; the people dug ditches in the roads and used cars as barriers. Aristide had ordered Blac to clear our zone.

At the same time the two electrical transformers in our zone had blown out, causing the whole zone to be in darkness. The Bale Wouze had also come into the zone and shot out all the street lamps. The people came to me and asked if YWAM could help with the transformers. We agreed, and together we were able to buy two transformers. We had gotten them just before the war broke out, but the electricity department (EDH) wouldn't come and install them because of all the problems. As a result, our zone was in total darkness through the night. This was one reason why the people had put up roadblocks. They didn't want the Bale Wouze coming in under the cover of darkness and shooting.

Blac had been ordered to clear the roadblocks in Portail Montrouis, as this zone was blocked out more than anywhere in the city. He beckoned me to him one day. "Terry, I want to let you know that tomorrow I am going to go into your zone and break down every roadblock, and I am going to 'eat people.' I'm telling you this so that you will stay in your mission. We don't want anyone to get hurt," he whispered.

I was shocked, desperately thinking of a way I could stop him from hurting our zone.

"Surely there must be a way around this," I pleaded.

"No, I have direct orders. I have to clear the roads tomorrow," he replied.

"Blac, what if I cleared the roads so that you wouldn't have to go through there and kill anybody," I said.

"You think you could do that?" he asked, surprised.

Not knowing whether I could, I confidently replied, "Yes, I can do it. Will you stay out of our zone if I do?"

"I don't have to pass through if the roads are cleared," he said.

We made a deal that if I would clear the roads by 8:00 AM, he would order EDH to come out and hang up the transformers in our zone so that we could have light. I went back to the zone and explained to everyone that Blac Ronald was planning to come in tomorrow and cause carnage. The people started screaming and panicking.

"But!" I said. "I have convinced him to stay out if we clear the roads. In exchange he will order the transformers to be put up so that we'll have light.

"We'll do it," they all said.

To be on the safe side, I told everyone the roads had to be cleared by 6:00 instead of 8:00.

The next morning I walked outside the base, and you would never have known there had been roadblocks. The roads were clear. By noon the EDH truck had finished hanging up the transformers, and our zone had electricity for the first time in months.

In the midst of everything, Lubens married Andie on January 24. I was Lubens' best man and even gave Andie away, as her father was no longer alive. It was a beautiful day—a moment of peace in the midst of a frightening time.

By February things were getting even more heated. The Bale Wouze attacked Ramicos, which used to be part of the Bale Wouze but had separated after a disagreement. The Bale Wouze killed many unarmed people at the Ramicos headquarters in La Scierie, where the flood had been. It was suspected that the attack was ordered by Aristide to rid the city of anyone in opposition to him. Shooting was going on throughout the city. Sporadically YWAMers had to duck and run as crossfire whistled through the base. At night the bullets would fall on our roof.

Meanwhile we were holding a Discipleship Training School. During heated times, we tried to maintain our focus on prayer. It became apparent that a point might come when we would need to evacuate. We held practice runs and used color codes for different types of evacuation. Everyone packed a suitcase, ready to leave at a moment's notice.

The pastors realized that some sort of resolution was needed between the Bale Wouze and Ramicos. The whole city was on fire, and people were arguing and fighting. One day I saw a pastor I knew jumping over our wall.

"What are you doing?" I asked.

"They're out to get me. They think I am against them," he said with a petrified look on his face. He was able to seek refuge on our campus for a while, escaping his attackers.

Pastors were in hiding, reporting that they couldn't sleep at night because of all the gunfighting. They tried to talk to the Bale Wouze and the Ramicos leaders but got nowhere.

Pierre-Richard and I went down to the wharf in the middle of all this to check on the work YWAM had been doing there.

"There's the député," Pierre-Richard said, pointing to a man in his late thirties standing by the wharf. Député Mayette had been voted in by Aristide's Lavalas party. He was given control of the city along with the Bale Wouze. I walked over to him, introduced myself, and explained the problems.

"We need to stop the shooting. What can we do?" I asked.

"I know who you are, and I can trust you. This is how we can bring it to a stop," he said.

He wanted Portail Montrouis to disarm. He asked me to relay the message to the zone. The people of our zone agreed, and I went back to tell the député.

"Great! The problems will now be resolved," he said, pleased.

"But I don't want any of your people coming into our zone with guns," I said.

He agreed. "I am going to put you in charge of your zone. You have my authorization to take guns from anybody you see in your zone who is carrying a gun."

I had found out that the Bale Wouze had put together a hit list of twenty-two men. The people on the list were part of Ramicos and people from our zone who were known to be able to shoot and were helping to smuggle guns to Gonaives. A man named Ti-Joe was one of the only surviving men from the list. He was a gunrunner and fixed guns by trade. He knew how to operate firearms, and he taught people how to shoot.

Ti-Joe had been caught in Terre Blanche, which means white earth (white dirt is everywhere in the area). He had gone to Terre Blanche to hide with two other people, one of whom was named Yveto. The Bale Wouze found out where they were hiding and raided the hideout. Ti-Joe just put his hands in the air, but Yveto ran. The Bale Wouze chased Yveto down. When they caught up with him, they shot him in the head.

This happened shortly after Mayette had told me that there would be no more guns and no more shooting. People from the zone came running to me to tell me that Yveto had been shot and killed and that Ti-Joe was in jail. I was sure it wasn't true, and although I hardly knew the guys at the time, I told the people I would check it out. They took me to Terre Blanche, where I asked the locals the details of how Yveto had died. I also asked them if there had been a gun battle.

The people began to talk, but then a man came and told them to be quiet. I could tell that everyone was extremely fearful. I saw the body of Yveto lying dead, covered with banana leaves. (The Bale Wouze never wanted to take the dead away. They wanted the dogs to eat them so that there would be no evidence.) I examined the body. Yveto's knees were bent, as if he had been kneeling face forward on the ground. I could see the hole in the top of his head where his brains had been blown out. It was clear it had been an execution.

When I came back, I met with our zone. I was overwhelmed with what had happened, and from seeing Yveto's dead body. The reality of what I had seen hit me, and I began to cry in front of the people and told them it was true—Yveto was dead.

"Ti-Joe is in jail. You have to help him," they said.

I decided to go to the police station and see if I could see Ti-Joe. But when I arrived, the guards wouldn't allow me in to see him.

All of a sudden the international press showed up at the prison. They had been tipped off that the police had caught an ex-senator hauling guns to Gonaives, trying to sneak them through St. Marc. His driver was being chased down in the mountains.

I was tempted to tell the international press about what had just happened in Terre Blanche.

Magistrat Ernest came up to my car.

"How are you?" he asked.

"Really bad," I replied, knowing from the people I had talked to that Ernest had been with Samoza's group that had executed Yveto. Ernest asked what I meant, so I told him what I knew. At first he tried to argue that a gun battle had taken place between his men and Yveto.

"Wouldn't these media people like to know what really went on?" I asked.

Magistrat Ernest froze.

I asked to talk to Mayette. Ernest said he was talking to reporters and couldn't come. Incensed, I again asked, "Wouldn't the reporters like to know what is really going on?"

That was enough for Ernest to draw Mayette aside and bring him to me.

"What's wrong?" Mayette asked, confused.

"Your men executed a man from my zone in Terre Blanche. I'm not happy about it," I told him.

At first Mayette pretended that this was news to him, but then he changed his tactics. "No, he was shooting at our guys, so they shot back and killed him," he said.

"No, he was executed. He got a bullet right in his head—he was on his knees," I responded.

I told Mayette that I needed him to allow me to go up to Terre Blanche to retrieve the body. At first Mayette refused. I applied some pressure, reminding him of the journalists present. Finally he submitted and let me go.

We went to Terre Blanche and got Yveto's body. It was the only one recovered from the twenty-two people on the hit list. We gave Yveto a proper funeral, although we had to do it in secret, since the Bale Wouze wanted to perform a voodoo ceremony on the body.

When I returned from Terre Blanche, I asked Mayette for Ti-Joe.

"But Ti-Joe is a gunrunner. Why do you want him?" he asked.

"He is from my zone. You told me I am responsible for everyone in my zone," I replied.

Mayette said he had been called for in Port-au-Prince. I said I didn't care who had called for him—he was from my zone and I wanted him. I again mentioned the media, which got Mayette's attention. Eventually Mayette said I could have Ti-Joe, but they would have to interrogate him first. I agreed.

A few hours after I had returned to the base, people from the zone came to me saying that the powers in Port-au-Prince had sent a helicopter to pick up Ti-Joe and take him back to the capital, where they felt sure he would be executed. As they were talking I heard the sound of a chopper whirring above the city. I immediately called Député Mayette and went to see him.

"If you do not give me Ti-Joe, you are going to have some serious problems," I said.

Mayette told me that I would get Ti-Joe after the interrogation. I knew that the helicopter was taking Ti-Joe to Port-au-Prince and that he was as good as dead. Mayette wasn't listening. Since I didn't know what else to do, I got up to leave. As soon as I began to walk out, Mayette picked up his phone.

I saw the helicopter return shortly afterward. Quickly I drove back to the police station and told Blac that the député had given me Ti-Joe.

"The député gave you Ti-Joe?" Blac asked incredulously.

"Yes. I am responsible for him. He's from my zone," I replied.

I walked back into the cells and saw Ti-Joe. He was very surprised to see me. I told him to hang on and that we were doing what we could.

Blac called Mayette, and sure enough he released Ti-Joe to me. Ti-Joe and I got in the car and headed for Portail Montrouis.

"Why did you do that?" Ti-Joe asked, sitting in the backseat, still shocked that he had been released.

I told him it was God who had released him.

"Can you pray for me, because I want to become a Christian. I know God saved me today, but I don't know why," he said humbly.

Ti-Joe told me that he had been taken up into the helicopter with two other prisoners. The Bale Wouze had put bags over their heads so that they couldn't see anything. Ti-Joe had sat on something lumpy. He kept losing his footing in the helicopter and was afraid he would fall out. Suddenly he was able to peek underneath the bag on his head. He realized he was sitting on human heads. He knew he was about to die.

All of a sudden Ti-Joe heard a thwack and a thump. The head of one of the other prisoners had been cut off and the body thrown out of the helicopter. The second prisoner was taken. He started pleading for his life. Thwack, his head came off as well. Ti-Joe knew that he was next. After a few moments the helicopter turned around and landed, and Ti-Joe was taken back to the prison.

"I asked myself why I was alive. Then you came to get me," he told me.

As we entered Portail Montrouis with Pierre-Richard, I suddenly felt the Lord say to turn around and go back. Instantly I turned the car around and started driving back. After a few moments, I saw a Bale

Wouze truck parked along the road. Two armed gunmen were standing next to the truck. I stopped the car and got out.

"What are you doing in our zone?" I asked.

They just looked at me as if to say, "Don't talk to us."

So I raised my voice. "What are you doing in our zone?" I repeated. I had learned that in Haiti you have to demand respect to gain respect. You can't speak softly. When you are talking to strong, hard men, you have to talk straight. "I am under the authorization of the député. He told me if I find any guns in my zone I am to seize them and take them to him. Give me your guns," I ordered.

All of a sudden six armed Bale Wouze members came out from behind the houses to the truck.

"What's going on? What's going on?" they screamed.

Samoza was leading the pack.

"What are you doing in my zone with guns?" I demanded.

"We are here on the député's business," he said.

"Not in my zone. If the député has business in my zone, he said he would contact me. He said I was to seize all guns. Give me your guns or leave this zone," I shouted. I was speaking some Creole, and Pierre-Richard was translating the rest.

Samoza stepped back, cocked the AK47 in his hand, and told all the men with him to be done with us, meaning to shoot us. All of a sudden the men surrounded Pierre-Richard and me, forming a circle around us. They cocked their guns as if to shoot.

*Lord, what do You want me to do?* I prayed desperately.

The Lord spoke clearly to my heart and mind: "Make a phone call."

I responded immediately. Just as in DTS when God had directed me to the broken truck, my obedience had to be instant and unquestioning. I pulled my phone out of my pocket and made out as if I were dialing, silently asking God who I was supposed to call.

"Hold the phone up in the air," I felt God say.

I held it up and said, "Go ahead and shoot. The whole world is listening."

I don't know where the words came from; they just came out of me.

The men looked at me and then at each other. Suddenly they lowered their guns.

"Let's get out of here," Samoza ordered. The men jumped into the back of the pickup truck with all their guns and sped away. My heart was racing a hundred miles an hour. As I watched them go I realized they were heading for our mission.

"Quick, get in the car," I screamed to Pierre-Richard.

Ti-Joe was sitting in shocked silence in the backseat.

We sped after the Bale Wouze, trying to get the mission on the phone to tell them to evacuate and close the gates. But we were too late. The Bale Wouze arrived at the mission and drove right into the driveway.

"They are going to attack the mission," I said, terrified.

All of a sudden they backed up and headed toward us at full speed.

"Hold your course," I felt God say.

*I've done this before,* I thought to myself. As a wild cowboy from Texas I had played chicken before. We would drive at each other head-on and see who would flinch first. I never would have guessed that that would be part of my mission training.

The truck came straight at us. I wondered whether we actually would collide, but I stayed the course. Suddenly inches from us they veered away and drove around us.

Pierre-Richard and I went straight into the base.

"Evacuation! Evacuation! Code blue!" I shouted. This meant that the base had fifteen minutes to get everything together and get out. I went to get all the business files from the office and ran over to my house. Ingvild already had the kids in the car.

"I didn't think this was going to happen. I don't know what to do," she said in a panic.

"You have to get out of here," I replied as firmly as I could.

"Try to get our pictures and some of our things if you can," she pleaded.

"I will, but you have to leave now," I said as I left the house and headed for the car. The kids were near to tears, but I tried to keep a brave face for them, holding back my own tears.

As I was saying my goodbyes, I tried to ignore the thought that this might be the last time I would ever see my family. I hugged Ingvild and told her that everything would be okay. They drove off, and I quickly ran into the house to get everything together. Brian said that we could try to get another vehicle out later with a trailer to haul some things of concern from the mission.

The DTS students were taken to a mission compound just outside Port-au-Prince. We had arranged for them to pass through the border with our vehicles into the Dominican Republic later on. Our intention was for the DTS to join the school in the Dominican Republic to complete their course. I had asked my family to go as well, but Ingvild felt that she and the children were supposed to stay. We had been serving in Haiti for thirteen years, and she said she was not about to leave at this crucial moment. She felt we were all called to stand as a family at this time and wait to see what the Lord would do.

There had been rumors that the powers in Port-au-Prince wanted me dead. Since people thought that they might try to get to me through Ingvild and the children, my family went into hiding. Many people were afraid to take them in, but eventually Ingvild and the children found safety in a mission in the mountains outside of Port-au-Prince. Ingvild had prayer times with the children, explaining things as they happened. Our children now have an understanding of God that is far beyond their age.

I had two hours to get everything I could think of into the few boxes we had. I had to pick things that would cause my family to remember me in case anything happened to me. It was very difficult.

By that evening we got the trailer out and reassessed the situation. Brian and I and a few Haitian staff members—Roberteau Desilorme, Fiance Alexi, Pierre-Richard Charlotin, and FanFan Poteau—were the only people left on the base. Brian left at about seven o'clock, just after dark, driving the trailer out of the city. The remaining staff members and I then came together. We all felt we were going to be attacked that night. In a somber mood we started to pray.

"What shall we do? What is God saying?" I asked the group.

"Everybody in our zone is preparing to leave," Pierre-Richard reported.

"Why?" I asked.

"They heard you had evacuated and said that if you're not going to be here, they're not going to stay, so they're leaving," he replied.

I knew this wasn't good for us or them.

We decided to go out into the zone to see what was going on. When we got to the front gate, people were walking down the road, pushing wheelbarrows holding everything they owned.

"What can we do, Pierre?" I asked.

"I don't know," he replied.

I decided to walk up the road so that people could see that I hadn't left. As I walked with Pierre-Richard, people started peering out of their doors and windows. I smiled and waved at them.

"*Béni soit l'Éternel!*" (Praise the Lord), I shouted to the people. As we walked down the middle of the road, hope came. Everyone began to praise God.

"Hello. Hallelujah! We are here. God's here," we shouted.

We walked the half mile to the market, and as we turned around to go back to the base, about 150 people had joined us. The crowd just grew and grew. By now it was nine o'clock and pitch black. Normally nobody would be out on the street at this time of night, but the street was filled with people praising God. Our praises became so triumphant that we couldn't even walk. We had to run and dance down the street. We had thought it was the end of our lives, and it had turned into a joyful celebration. Cries of *"Béni soit l'Éternel!"* filled the streets.

When we got back to the base, people didn't want to stop. I knew they would have gone on all night.

"I'm not leaving. I am going to stay here with you," I told the people.

"Then we will stay too," they shouted.

I prayed a prayer over the zone.

"Now we can all go to sleep in peace," I said as I finished, and everyone dispersed back to his house, happy and laughing.

"That was God," Pierre said, laughing as the last of the people left.

We went back in the gate and prayed. We were ready for anyone to come in at any time.

Morning came and nothing had happened.

It was during this time that I heard the angels in our house protecting me. That word from God and the vision of the angels from YWAM India greatly encouraged me. I had received word of rumors that the president wanted me dead. I was messing up his plans in St. Marc, and it was said he wanted me out of the way. I knew this was serious. We had stepped up security on the base: we always had a person on watch throughout the night and kept the electric fence on. But in the end I knew that if the president's men were coming to get me, they would get me. God was showing me that the angels were with me, and that gave me peace.

Every night we would hear gunshots, and every day we would go out to see what had happened, trying to make communication with the Bale Wouze. We would sometimes go and share the gospel with them, giving them Bibles. One day they would be trying to kill us; the next day we were eating with them. It made no sense. Many of them were hooked on drugs, and when they were high, they became very dangerous. We tried to avoid them at these times.

We would visit different zones and try to assess the situation. We went through our zone to the street vendors, buying huge pots of food to distribute. God opened the hearts of businessmen. One man who felt God tell him we would need money gave $10,000. We went to the flood victims, knowing that they had no resources to fall back on because the flood had taken everything. We made cash donations if they had an ID card. We gave each person a hundred gourdes, which was about $US12. This goes a long way in Haiti. The bank was so supportive that if I needed money and it was closed, I could call the director, who had given me his personal cell phone number, and he would open the bank and withdraw money for me. He knew that it wasn't safe for me to have money outside, and he also knew that if I needed money, it was for the people.

We fed our zone for two weeks through the street vendors. It seemed like we never slept.

One evening after witnessing too many of the atrocities of war, I'd had enough. I cried out to God, saying it was too hard. I couldn't stay any longer. I went home, took a shower, and got into clothes I would wear to leave the city. I got my bag and met Pierre-Richard downstairs. It was midnight. We both knew it would be too dangerous to leave in the dark, so I settled down on the sofa and tried to sleep.

Early the next morning I checked my e-mails. One was from my dad, who had no idea of the struggle I was going through at the time. He began by saying he felt it was time I knew something. This caught my attention. He told me a story about my grandfather, the Reverend Latin Snow. Poppy Snow had been persecuted for helping black people in South Texas. He had given food to the people and had challenged his church to help by also giving. Because of this he wasn't served at certain grocery stores and endured constant abuse, even being voted out of the church where he was pastor. One evening in frustration he stayed up all night praying. God spoke to him, saying that through his grandchildren He would bless the black race. I was touched deeply. The e-mail gave me the strength to stand another day.

# SEVENTEEN

# Strength through Humility

DURING this time I was on the phone often with different intercessors from around the world. I sent out e-mail alerts two or three times a day, telling people where I was and what was going on so that they would know how to pray. God was using Alistair Petrie to give me guidance. Originally from Scotland but now living in Canada, Alistair was the man who had given me the word when I was in Jamaica that my life could be in danger.

I had called Alistair on the day of the Samoza incident, describing how I had knelt on the ground and Samoza had put the gun to my head. Alistair was very encouraging. He explained the principle behind why we had not been shot and had been able to walk away. Through the act of humility, by bowing down, we had broken the strongman that was being manifested through Samoza. Because the fear that Samoza was trying to bestow on people was not materializing, the back of the enemy had been broken. The key was showing humility, praying, and repenting for sins.

That night, all the pastors rallied together at a scheduled prayer meeting at the base. I told them what had happened and felt that God had led us to talk about the importance of repentance. We all needed to repent for the sins of the city. It was through acts of humility that the course of the city and the war would change.

The pastors tried to repent, but something was not breaking.

"God," I cried out, "what can be done? These pastors are trying, but they need help. They need the Holy Spirit."

"You repent," God replied.

"Me?" I said. "What did I do?"

God told me to model repentance, to demonstrate it. I asked the pastors to forgive the white race for the oppression we had brought to Haiti from slavery, when we had beaten and abused their forefathers. As I began to pray out repentance, God hit me with an overwhelming heart of humility. I ended up weeping and bowing on my knees before the pastors. My heart was so heavy-laden with the sins of my people that I knew that God was doing something through me.

All the pastors gathered around me and spontaneously prayed for healing as they laid their hands on me. They prayed for forgiveness. Two pastors picked me up off the floor. "Don't kneel anymore. There is no need for you to kneel. Rise up. You are our brother," they said.

One pastor bowed before me on his hands and knees. He confessed the sins of Haiti against the white race, how the people had attacked and killed innocent women and children, how they had cut off white people's heads and planted them on stakes throughout the land as a symbol that the white race would always be their enemy. They asked for forgiveness for how they were currently treating the white people, how they hadn't accepted missionaries but had taken advantage of them.

It was a powerful time. At the end we asked God to forgive and cleanse Haiti. We held hands and said one final prayer, and the meeting was over. I had been ready to stay for several hours in prayer, but it was all done in half an hour, and the air was clear. Our hearts were light, and we knew we had accomplished what God had wanted us to accomplish.

From that night on we never heard another shot during the night. We believed that the stronghold had been broken.

The next day I asked God where I was supposed to go and what I was supposed to do. It occurred to me that I had gone to the enemy's camp, to the police and the Bale Wouze, and had told them to repent, but I hadn't given them the chance to repent. So Pierre-Richard and I went back to the police. We talked to them and let them know that we were there if they wanted to pray with us. For the first time we noticed that Aristide's men were all wearing brand-new crucifixes. A fear of God was in the camp, and the men were trying to protect themselves from the wrath of God.

When we showed up at the Bale Wouze headquarters, Samoza was standing there. He signaled to me to come to him, and he drew me off to a quiet, secluded area.

"I want you to know, I will never touch you. You have nothing to worry about from me," he said in perfect English. As he spoke, tears welled up in his eyes. If there ever was an act of repentance, that would have probably been the greatest I had ever seen.

I never saw him in any aggression after that. The war ended, with Aristide leaving the country, and all his men left St. Marc early in the morning. Some caught boats, others jumped on trucks headed for Port-au-Prince.

When the city found that the Bale Wouze were gone, there was much celebration. We drove through the city, and the people jumped on our car, parading us as victors. Suddenly as we were driving into our zone, we saw people carrying a huge blue and red Haitian flag. As we drove, they raised the flag and let it fall over our car, covering us completely. After a few seconds, they lifted the flag up, and we drove on. This was a sign of the people's acceptance and thanks for all we had done.

As the day went on, the peaceful celebration turned to vengeance. All the people who had been attacked by the Bale Wouze went to take revenge in places where any relative of the Bale Wouze lived or worked. They attacked Samoza's mother's restaurant, which was by the wharf where the boats came into St. Marc. The restaurant was also next to a place called the "parking," where imported goods and vehicles were kept until cleared by customs.

I felt I should find out what was going on. A gang of two hundred were burning the restaurant. They had taken out all the bottles of cold drinks and were smashing them against the cement walls one by one. Pierre-Richard and I walked right into the attack. I felt like I was in a den of raging lions, only I was untouched. The attackers' eyes were glazed over, almost as if they weren't seeing what they were doing.

"You can't do anything. You're going to get hurt," Pierre-Richard said, beckoning to me to get out.

I started to leave, but then we saw that the mob was heading for the parking to steal and destroy what was stored inside. I knew that the vehicles and possessions of innocent people were stored there because of the war.

"This can't happen," I said.

I stood in front of the gate as the mob headed our way.

"Lord, help me," I quickly prayed.

Scores of angry people pressed against me, pushing me into the gate. They were screaming at me to get out of the way so that they could break the gate down.

"I am going to die before I let you in there to destroy anything," I said.

I just stood, feeling the pressure on my body as they pushed against me. Finally I realized there was no way I could stop them. I bowed my head and started praying.

"God, I speak peace in this place."

All of a sudden I felt the pressure lessen on me. I continued praying, and in a little while I looked up and saw that the crowd had dispersed. Only about fifty people were left, waiting to see what would happen.

A man came up to me and handed me the key to the gate. I opened it up, went inside, and quickly locked the gate again. I wanted to see how I could keep the place safe. I phoned some friends who worked as security guards and asked them to help secure the parking. I couldn't offer them money, but they agreed to come and secure it anyway. Many of the owners of the vehicles had heard about the mob and came to see the damage. When they saw everything untouched, they were thankful. I was able to tell them that God had saved their vehicles.

After several days we heard that the people had caught Samoza. I knew that he'd be dead if I didn't get to him. I heard that he was in a vehicle headed for St. Marc. He had been caught in a city about an hour south of St. Marc. I got in my car and headed for the outskirts of the city, hoping to cut them off. I knew that if they entered the city, Samoza would be dead. As I was driving through St. Marc, it looked like a giant parade. All the people were lined up along the street. I called the U.S. Embassy to tell them that Samoza had been caught and that we needed military immediately, as I felt the city was about to be turned upside down. While I was on the phone, three cars sped past me into St. Marc. Samoza was in one of them. I turned my car around to give them chase. As we came closer to the center of town, people started closing in around the cars.

Samoza was taken to the Ramicos headquarters. He was found guilty of being the instigator of the major massacre at La Scierie, where the Ramicos headquarters were. He had spilled much blood. When they got him to the Ramicos headquarters, he was almost dead. He had been shot through the cheek while in the car. Later I found out that it had been an accident. Barely conscious, Samoza was taken back to the place of his crime with another sidekick, Armstrong.

I stopped my car and pushed through the crowd. Tens of thousands of people had come out to witness the killing of Samoza. Thinking I wanted to be a part of what was happening, everyone was shouting, "Let Terry through." All I wanted was to pray with Samoza and make sure he was saved. But I was too late. The angry crowd had already severed his head from his body. I saw Samoza's headless body being beaten with machetes. I turned and walked away, knowing there was nothing I could do.

The crowd ended up cutting Samoza's body into many parts, tying ropes to each part and running through the city to show the people that he was dead.

Later we heard that before being captured, Samoza had gone to his sister's house to find refuge. His sister had given him a room and said he came out only to go to the bathroom. On the day he was captured he said he was going back to St. Marc.

"Don't do that. They'll surely kill you," his sister had pleaded.

"Everything is okay. Don't worry about me," Samoza had said, handing her the Bible I had given him.

We hope and pray that Samoza made his peace with God.

Aristide left the country on the first of March, and my family returned with some other staff members a week later.

# EIGHTEEN

# Seven Spheres
# of Influence

WHEN we first arrived in Haiti we had asked God to show us how we could impact the nation for Him. Because we didn't want to be just stereotypical missionaries, we asked Him for a strategy to transform Haiti. As we pioneered the base in St. Marc, God began to speak to us about the seven spheres of influence in a society: the church or religion; education; family or social groups; government; business; entertainment, including arts and sports; and the media. We felt that God was saying that if we touched all seven spheres, we would impact the city and then the nation. Youth With A Mission has been anointed to reach the lost through evangelism, training, and mercy ministry, which would be our tools to influence the spheres.

At first we felt that if we could impact just one sphere we would be able to make a dent in the community of St. Marc. But we found that by penetrating one, two, three, or even six of the seven spheres of influence, we still could not change the course of the city, let alone the whole nation. All seven spheres had to be impacted before we could make a substantial difference in a community.

God showed us that we had to look for the gatekeeper of each sphere. We asked Him to highlight the person to us. Once we had gained favor and trust with the gatekeeper, we had an open door to influence the sphere. It is important to note that nothing can change without the power and anointing of God. Without God's favor and help we would never have been able to touch the seven spheres, let alone impact the city. "'Not by might nor by power, but by my Spirit,' says the LORD Almighty" (Zechariah 4:6).

## CHURCH

Implementing the seven spheres kicked off after I got out of prison. It started with the church. We were able for the first time to rally the pastors, representing over twenty thousand people. As the church began to gain influence in St. Marc, we knew we had to work to rebuild its integrity. We did this through mercy ministry, building the gate and monument, and digging wells. People were not used to the church giving. As a result of the restored integrity, the pastors were able to have a platform and a voice. The church in St. Marc is once again speaking out as the moral conscience of the community, and people are now listening. The voice of the church is becoming louder than the voice of voodoo.

## EDUCATION

The sphere of education taught us an important lesson in looking for the gatekeeper. God revealed the person to us, and it wasn't whom we expected. The gatekeeper for education in St. Marc was the city's administrator, who was a part-time teacher. Getting to know him and gaining his trust were imperative to influencing the schools for Christ.

Brian Shipley founded our own school, Liberty Academy, in 1994. Through the school we wanted to model what an educational system could be. We began to give the teachers in the community seminars and training. The teachers in St. Marc respected us now that we had become educators ourselves.

After my imprisonment, our connection with the schools grew through the pastors' network. Most of the pastors had some connection with a school. With their help we held a seminar on education at which two hundred teachers participated.

After training in the United States, Illioney St. Fleur became the new director of Liberty Academy in 2004. He now holds seminars for teachers from various schools. Through our school we want to teach the children to reason, deduct, and conclude, rather than just memorize facts, which is the standard method of teaching in Haitian schools. We are encouraging students to think for themselves. We know that education is more than just academic achievement or rote memorization; it is about the formation of character.

## FAMILY

The family structure is so broken down in Haiti that it doesn't have a mother-father-child emblem. The Haitian community is formed in clusters or clans, with the cluster or clan working together to discipline or take care of a child. There are still mother/father influences, but the family structure is broader. A whole zone would consider itself one family.

We used mercy ministry to gain influence. This gave us an opening to teach a whole family of people how to live according to biblical values and principles as well as the opportunity to share the gospel and win people to Christ. This was highlighted during the war. Our zone adopted us into their family because I didn't leave. This spoke volumes to the people, and as a result they asked me to preach to them night after night. Many came to us after the war saying that their children would have died of hunger if YWAM had not fed them through the street vendors.

## GOVERNMENT

We used mercy ministry again as a tool to appeal to the mayor to fix the fountain in the park. By doing this we gained influence, insight, and trust, which developed further after that. One day the mayor asked us if we could go to La Grange, a remote village on the outskirts of the city and a place that the government had forgotten. La Grange was a community of about two thousand people. When we got there, it was as if we had stumbled onto a poor African village. Naked children were running around, the people lived in mud huts, and the place was covered with dirt and dust. There was no clean water—only a muddy river where the cows bathed and the people drank from. The area had an 80 percent infant mortality rate for children under two, mostly caused by diarrhea.

We were immediately able to give the people water filters, and later we drilled a well for them. As a result we gained trust and influence. During 2004 our bond with the mayor grew even closer. At one point his life was in danger: the Bale Wouze were after him because he had refused to come under their authority. He asked Youth With A Mission to help him, and we sneaked him out of the city to save his life.

After the war the next administration saw the good works we had done with the former mayor and called upon our assistance. They said it was apparent that Youth With A Mission was more effective than they were in influencing the city. This was only by the grace of God.

## BUSINESS

In business we had a little influence through friendship. Mercy ministry does not apply to economics, because these people are making money. We had to ask God to show us how to influence business in St. Marc. Our opportunity came through our influence in the government. Government officials had asked us to help run the beef and fish market in the heart of the city. We agreed to help for a contracted five years. This was our chance to gain influence and reach the business sector. Before this time, businessmen would talk to us as if we didn't understand them. We had tried to set up Bible studies for the businessmen we knew, but we hadn't been able to break through. Now that we are running the market, the businessmen talk to us eye to eye. They feel we understand them. We are equals. The market has made it possible for us to disciple and challenge businessmen on how they conduct their businesses and to give out of their businesses to see the city improve and develop.

Since Youth With A Mission is a nonprofit organization, we approach the market from a teaching, training, and health-care perspective. Any economic benefit we might get is committed to go back into the development of the market.

## ENTERTAINMENT, ARTS, AND SPORTS

Because the arts and entertainment of Haiti was overridden with voodoo and immoral images, we weren't sure how we could use it for the gospel. First we challenged the churches to clean up and repaint their buildings. We sent YWAM teams to help the poorer churches. We also put up the monument in the park, a specific attempt to try to capture the arts. We held concerts of Christian groups and choirs at our facility, and we showed films, like *The Passion of the Christ,* to give an alternative form of entertainment. The soccer matches we held on the YWAM campus were also instrumental in influencing this sphere.

## MEDIA

We decided to start filming our crusades and showing them on television. The only TV station in St. Marc gave us a price for broadcasting the event. After they suggested a large fee, I bargained with them, as is customary in the culture, and brought the price down. When I got the price I was happy with, we went ahead with the filming. The station did a good job, and I felt God speak to me about being generous to them. Even though we didn't have much money, I knew I had to be obedient. As soon as the job was done, I went to pay my bill. I not only paid the bill but also gave them an additional amount. I ended up paying what they had originally asked for. I also tipped the cameramen. This shocked both the cameramen and the producers, who never expected Christians to be generous and to give over and above what was expected.

As a result, at one of our crusades the TV producer began listening to the preaching. Toward the end of the night he came up to me. "Terry, your message is something I have never heard of before. It has touched my heart," he said.

"Would you like to accept Christ?" I asked.

He said yes, and he became a Christian.

We won the television media through mercy ministry, giving freely, and sharing the gospel with them, winning them to Christ. Now if I need a message communicated over television, I can call on my Christian brother, and in fifteen minutes he will provide a cameraman anywhere in the city. In one to two hours I can have the message being broadcast on the air. This is a powerful tool that we have been able to capitalize on.

It is the same story with the radio. The radio station staff asked us to help them learn English. We immediately agreed and made good friends with them.

Once we began to influence these seven areas, we could "capture" the city. We then had the authority to look at what was wrong in the city and seek to change it for the better. Once we captured St. Marc, our aim was to disciple the city through evangelism, training, and mercy ministry.

We asked God to show us His destiny for the city. The name St. Marc is from the gospel of Mark, which talks about the first acts of Christ. We believe the first acts of transformation in the nation of Haiti will come from St. Marc. Recently a U.S. consul general passed through the city. He was impressed by what he saw in St. Marc. "It seems to me that St. Marc may become a model to the nation," he said.

When Pastor Chavanne Jeune, a presidential candidate for the 2006 elections, came to St. Marc, he was touched by the monument of the Ten Commandments in the park. He said that if he was elected, he would place similar monuments throughout the nation during his first ninety days in office.

The word of what is happening in St. Marc has spread through Haiti like wildfire. Even though people don't know all the details, they do know that profound changes are taking place in the city. St. Marc is demonstrating God's transforming power in Haiti.

Youth With A Mission has now expanded to Gonaives and another city, Jacmel, in the south. In each city, we go through the same process of trying to influence the seven spheres to make an impact for God. The YWAM director in Gonaives, Maula Jean-Marie, got a word from the Lord about the destiny for his city that sums up what we are all asking God to do: *Heal the city, touch the nation, win the world.*

# NINETEEN

# A Curse Overcome

AFTER the war the city had no leadership or government. Because they had seen how God had worked through us during the war, many city leaders came to YWAM during that time, asking us how they should run the city.

Because of what God had done through us, the people wanted to elevate YWAM and give us a "crown." We felt like we had to do what Jesus did when at different times the people came to crown Him as King of the Jews. He disappeared, hiding from the crowd. We knew we had to do the same. We could not receive any glory for ourselves for what God had done.

Some of the Ramicos leaders in the city approached us and asked what they should do with regard to the amount of blood that had been spilled in the city. Since as pastors we had repented during the war, I sensed the need for the whole city to repent, and I suggested that we call for a day of repentance.

"That's it! That's what we need," they responded immediately.

The Ramicos leaders had asked for all the schools and businesses to reopen on Monday, March 8. As we talked about repentance, they felt that they should first set aside a day for a time of prayer over their city. The people could then ask God to forgive their sins and the blood that was shed. The Ramicos leaders asked me if I would help coordinate the religious leaders in a day of prayer and repentance. They asked me if I would bring the Catholic and Protestant churches together. I was excited but overwhelmed by this idea. To my knowledge the Protestant and Catholic ministries in Haiti had never come together in unity for a purpose such as this. As usual I had no idea how this would happen, but I immediately told the leaders that I would do it.

We had a pastors' meeting that evening. The pastors were unanimous in their support. I went to see the Catholic priest to explain our idea and asked if his church would join us. "You know the sins that have been committed in the city. You know the blood that has been spilled. We need a day of prayer and repentance," I said. "Would you join us?"

The Catholic priest was humbled. "Of course we will stand with you," he replied.

The day of repentance dawned, starting with a mass at the Catholic church. The mass was a memorial service for all who were killed in the war. The priest spoke to the congregation, explaining that our job, as those still living, was to move on by forgiving. In the afternoon the people met at the steps of the city hall. We had been given a huge sound system designed to reach approximately ten thousand people. The system had been donated by Claire Brothers, a music business in Pennsylvania. We set it up so that the multitudes of people who were coming could hear what was going on.

About two o'clock we gathered in front of the city hall. The stage was set, the sound system was in place, and our program was ready. All the pastors had gathered in the city hall to pray. The most senior pastor in the network, Pastor Xavier, led us all in communion. As we stepped outside, I gasped to see the streets filled with thousands of people. There were so many that we had to set up some small PA speakers at the edge of the city park to broadcast even farther out to those on the outskirts.

The police diverted the traffic from Route National One that passed in front of the park to eliminate any congestion or noise that might disturb the time of prayer.

The pastors made their way onto the platform.

People kept on coming until the park was completely filled. The Catholic priest stepped up to the microphone. "Never before have I been so blessed to be a part of something so significant in the history of our nation," he said with tears in his eyes.

His words stuck in my heart. The atmosphere in the place was electric. People had turned out in their Sunday best. They were all silent, still shell-shocked from the experiences of the past few weeks.

The priest led a prayer of blessing, asking God to forgive us. Two nuns stood to the left and the right of the priest, and all three prayed out prayers over the city, asking God to heal and bless the land.

Then it was my turn to speak. I had no idea what to say, but God suddenly brought the word *foundation* to my mind. I recalled the verse God had given us from Zechariah 8:9–13. I told the people we needed to lay a solid foundation in the city of St. Marc for a future of prosperity and growth. I focused on the Ten Commandments and directed people's attention toward the park. As I was preaching I felt God challenge me to tell something of the history of St. Marc.

I asked the people to forgive my race as I stood as a white man before them in the city park. Two hundred years ago, after they had begun to pull their troops out, the French had called for the Haitian slaves who had joined arms to fight alongside them to gather in the center of the park. They lured them there with the understanding that they were going to be honored in some special way. As the Haitians waited in the center of the park, some troops from Poland came in and surrounded the slaves. The Haitians inside the circle wondered what was happening. Then the French made an outer circle around the Polish soldiers and ordered them to open fire on the slaves. If any slaves trying to flee for their lives made it through the circle of Polish troops, the French would finish them off before they could escape. This had all happened in the city park.

I felt that before I could continue to speak about repentance, I had to ask for forgiveness and repent for the sins of the white race. After I did this, there seemed to be a breaking in the spiritual realm. An attitude of humility came to the crowd. People had come to repent, and they were now being asked to forgive. Once again God seemed to be using me to model repentance. This was well received, and the people responded by saying they forgave me.

During the war there had been hardly any rain. The park was mostly dried up apart from one green spot surrounding the monument of the Ten Commandments. This could not be explained. Also during the war every building in the city had been covered with graffiti, but the monument was untouched. And although the whole city was riddled with bullet holes, not one bullet had hit the monument. We recognized that God had been there and God was with us. He was pointing to His word, showing the people that His word is life.

After I had spoken they called Ti-Joe, who told how God had delivered him and that he was now a Christian. Ti-Joe said he had forgiven those who had tried to kill him. His life was a challenge to the people of St. Marc. The people were open-mouthed at his words.

On the outskirts of our city in an area called Pierre Payen was a huge lake full of fish. In 2002 the water had started decreasing and was dwindling away. By the end of the year, the lake had completely dried up. During the war it was so dry that I was able to drive across it looking for people who were under attack or had been killed.

I could never figure out what had caused the lake to dry up. No one could explain it. We had the same amount of rain as usual, even a flood in St. Marc, but mysteriously the lake had disappeared. No one could recall such a thing ever happening before. After the day of repentance, rain began to fall. All of a sudden the lake held water; it was filled to two-thirds. It didn't go dry again. The next year it filled fuller. It is now almost completely full. As I read 2 Chronicles 7:14—"If my people...will humble themselves...and turn from their wicked ways, then will I hear from heaven...and will heal their land"—I feel we saw a small part of this healing come to pass.

With this vision of Haiti's healing, we were able with God's help to put together an event in November 2004. We called it "Haiti, You Are a Voice, Not an Echo." People from nations from around the world, including South Africa, Venezuela, Israel, the Dominican Republic, Jamaica, Lebanon, Europe, Canada, and the United States, arrived to attend. Eighteen different nationalities and twenty-one languages were represented at the event.

We felt it was important to hold the event in Port-au-Prince, since it is the capital of Haiti. The different nations spoke to Haiti prophetically through the arts, through song, and through dance that God has a destiny for the people and nation of Haiti. Haiti would fulfill its destiny and no longer be an echo but would be a voice in the nations.

The climax of the event came when we were invited to the presidential palace. We were taken into the room where all the past presidents had been inaugurated. We had a time of celebration, prayer, and dancing. The King's Kids (a youth evangelistic group) from YWAM Gonaives came and put on a drama showing how freedom comes from within through the power of God. Suddenly President Boniface Alexandre came forward and thanked the nations for coming in and praying over the palace and the government.

At the end of the event, the nations gave gifts to the president. One man by the name of Armando Benner, a Venezuelan Jew, came forward and said, "Mr. President, I would like to give you a gift on behalf of my country and my cultural roots." He then handed the president a blue and white Israeli flag and a small vial of olive oil used for anointing for healing. As President Alexandre opened his hands to receive the gifts, Armando placed a small portion of the oil on the president's hands and prayed that God would use the president to begin to bring healing to the land. This was profound. Never before in the history of the nation had a president in Haiti been prayed over in such a manner.

What was amazing was that a Canadian intercessor, who did not know the history of Haiti, had had a vision which she described to me. She had seen a cup filled with pigs' blood pass from president to president. Then she saw the president's hands being anointed with oil, which broke the curse, and the cup of blood fell to the ground. This sent ricochets through the nation as people began to hear that their president had been prayed over by a Jew who had asked God to bring healing to the land. Many people said that surely this had broken the curse from the presidency of Haiti. We were excited that God used the event and specifically the anointing in that way.

One of the Haitian King's Kids spoke after the event. "As a child I had always seen so many terrible things from our government that I was not excited to visit the palace. I saw it as a place of evil where terrible things had happened. But being here now has shown me that God can heal a nation. Now I am proud to have been in our palace."

As we reflect how over the years God has taken us from nothing to praying in the presidential palace, the words of Revelation 12:11 have become reality for us: "They overcame him by the blood of the Lamb and by the word of their testimony; they did not love their lives so much as to shrink from death."

These three things—the blood, the word of our testimony, and not loving our lives even to the point of death—have been key for us in finding the victory, courage, and strength to continue to believe God for the transformation of this nation.

# About the Author

JEMIMAH WRIGHT has worked with YWAM in Hawaii, the Philippines, and Haiti. She studied at Oxford Brookes University, spent a year in Cape Town helping children affected by AIDS, and then returned to England to train as a journalist. Jemimah lives in Bristol, England, and works as a freelance journalist.

# International Adventures

### Lords of the Earth, by Don Richardson

Engulfed in the darkness of Irian Jaya's Snow Mountains lived the Yali—cannibals who called themselves "lords of the earth." Missionary Stan Dale dared to enter their domain. 978-1-57658-290-9

### Bruchko, by Bruce Olson

The astonishing true story of a nineteen-year-old's capture by the Stone Age Motilone Indians in a South American jungle and the impact he had living out the gospel among them. 978-1-57658-348-7

### A Cry from the Streets, by Jeannette Lukasse

A dramatic story of rescue and restoration unfolds when a young couple goes to live among the street children of Brazil. 978-1-57658-263-3

### Imprisoned in Iran, by Dan Baumann

Wrongly accused of espionage and thrown into the most infamous high-security prison in Iran, one American man witnessed the powerful triumph of God's love over fear. 978-1-57658-180-3

### Torches of Joy, by John Dekker with Lois Neely

In one generation, the Dani people of Irian Jaya took the dangerous leap from the Stone Age into the twentieth century, discovering the gospel of Jesus and their destiny as His helpers. 978-0-927545-43-3

### The Man with the Bird on His Head, by John Rush and Abbe Anderson

A converted atheist on a medical mission may be the mysterious messenger predicted by the prophecies of a Pacific cult and the key to reaching an island with the gospel. 978-1-57658-005-9

### Living on the Devil's Doorstep, by Floyd McClung

From the hippie trail through Kabul, Afghanistan, to the infamous red light district of Amsterdam, a young couple steps out in faith with the message of hope. 978-0-927545-45-7

### Against All Odds, by Jim Stier

The story of one man's dedicated passion for the people of Brazil is a compelling reminder that God restores broken lives and broken dreams. 978-0-927545-44-0

### Tomorrow You Die, by Reona Peterson Joly

Facing the ultimate risk, two women obey God's call to bring the gospel to the people of Albania. 978-0-927545-92-1

### Dayuma: Life under Waorani Spears, by Ethel Emily Wallis

The story of the five missionary martyrs in Ecuador comes full circle in the breathtaking true story of Dayuma, who left her tribe on a desperate odyssey into the unknown. 978-0-927545-91-4

### Adventures in Naked Faith, by Ross Tooley

Stories from the Philippines bring a challenge to a deeper, tested faith that will change believers' lives and the lives of those they encounter. 978-0-927545-90-7

### Totally Surrounded, by Christina Di Stefano Davis

Surrounded by militant rebels, witch doctors, and the Philippine jungle, one woman relentlessly proclaimed the transforming power of God. 978-1-57658-165-0

### Walking Miracle, by Art Sanborn

After years serving on the Asian mission field, Art Sanborn would rely on the power of Jesus in a new way when doctors told him he would never walk again. 978-1-57658-455-2

# Christian Heroes: Then & Now

*Adventure-filled Christian biographies for ages 10 to 100!*

Readers of all ages love the exciting, challenging, and deeply touching true stories of ordinary men and women whose trust in God accomplished extraordinary exploits for His kingdom and glory.

*Gladys Aylward: The Adventure of a Lifetime* • *978-1-57658-019-6*
*Nate Saint: On a Wing and a Prayer* • *978-1-57658-017-2*
*Hudson Taylor: Deep in the Heart of China* • *978-1-57658-016-5*
*Amy Carmichael: Rescuer of Precious Gems* • *978-1-57658-018-9*
*Eric Liddell: Something Greater Than Gold* • *978-1-57658-137-7*
*Corrie ten Boom: Keeper of the Angels' Den* • *978-1-57658-136-0*
*William Carey: Obliged to Go* • *978-1-57658-147-6*
*George Müller: Guardian of Bristol's Orphans* • *978-1-57658-145-2*
*Jim Elliot: One Great Purpose* • *978-1-57658-146-9*
*Mary Slessor: Forward into Calabar* • *978-1-57658-148-3*
*David Livingstone: Africa's Trailblazer* • *978-1-57658-153-7*
*Betty Greene: Wings to Serve* • *978-1-57658-152-0*
*Adoniram Judson: Bound for Burma* • *978-1-57658-161-2*
*Cameron Townsend: Good News in Every Language* • *978-1-57658-164-3*
*Jonathan Goforth: An Open Door in China* • *978-1-57658-174-2*
*Lottie Moon: Giving Her All for China* • *978-1-57658-188-9*
*John Williams: Messenger of Peace* • *978-1-57658-256-5*
*William Booth: Soup, Soap, and Salvation* • *978-1-57658-258-9*
*Rowland Bingham: Into Africa's Interior* • *978-1-57658-282-4*
*Ida Scudder: Healing Bodies, Touching Hearts* • *978-1-57658-285-5*
*Wilfred Grenfell: Fisher of Men* • *978-1-57658-292-3*
*Lillian Trasher: The Greatest Wonder in Egypt* • *978-1-57658-305-0*
*Loren Cunningham: Into All the World* • *978-1-57658-199-5*
*Florence Young: Mission Accomplished* • *978-1-57658-313-5*
*Sundar Singh: Footprints Over the Mountains* • *978-1-57658-318-0*
*C. T. Studd: No Retreat* • *978-1-57658-288-6*
*Rachel Saint: A Star in the Jungle* • *978-1-57658-337-1*
*Brother Andrew: God's Secret Agent* • *978-1-57658-355-5*
*Clarence Jones: Mr. Radio* • *978-1-57658-343-2*
*Count Zinzendorf: Firstfruit* • *978-1-57658-262-6*
*John Wesley: The World His Parish* • *978-1-57658-382-1*
*C. S. Lewis: Master Storyteller* • *978-1-57658-385-2*
*David Bussau: Facing the World Head-on* • *978-1-57658-415-6*
*Jacob DeShazer: Forgive Your Enemies* • *978-1-57658-475-0*
*Isobel Kuhn: On the Roof of the World* • *978-1-57658-497-2*
*Elisabeth Elliot: Joyful Surrener* • *978-1-57658-513-9*